"Jonathan Edward⌐ ⌐ver produced. I once took an entire year to read through his complete body of work. The wisdom was staggering. Now, another brilliant mind, my dear friend Kyle Strobel, has made Edwards accessible to everyone, on the critical issue of spiritual formation through godly habits and attitudes. This is an important book that can change your life."

Rick Warren, Saddleback Church

"If you are among those either unacquainted with Jonathan Edwards or simply afraid to read him, this book is for you. As best I can tell, what Kyle Strobel has done here is largely unprecedented in Edwardsean studies. With Edwards as tour guide, he has taken us on a journey, both deeply theological and eminently practical, into what it means to live Christianly. If biblical spirituality is something you cherish and long for, you can do no better than join Strobel, together with Edwards, in this profoundly life-changing exploration. Highly recommended!"

Sam Storms, Lead Pastor, Bridgeway Church, Oklahoma City

"We sometimes imagine that 'spiritual formation'—the Spirit's work of conforming us to the image of God's Son—is something accomplished on our own. But in reality, God has graciously given us the gift of teachers and the community of saints. These wise guides can lead us and help us, through their teaching and example, pointing us to Christ. We could not ask for a more profound guide than the great theologian Jonathan Edwards. In these pages his gifted interpreter Kyle Strobel shows us a better way—a way less traveled—for how to live the Christian life bound to the Son in love. A feast awaits all those with eyes to see."

Justin Taylor, managing editor, *The ESV Study Bible*; coeditor (with John Piper), *A God-Entranced Vision of All Things*

FORMED FOR THE GLORY OF GOD

LEARNING FROM THE SPIRITUAL PRACTICES OF JONATHAN EDWARDS

KYLE STROBEL

IVP Books

An imprint of InterVarsity Press
Downers Grove, Illinois

InterVarsity Press
P.O. Box 1400, Downers Grove, IL 60515-1426
World Wide Web: www.ivpress.com
Email: email@ivpress.com

InterVarsity Press® is the book-publishing division of InterVarsity Christian Fellowship/USA®, a
movement of students and faculty active on campus at hundreds of universities, colleges and schools of
nursing in the United States of America, and a member movement of the International Fellowship of
Evangelical Students. For information about local and regional activities, write Public Relations Dept.,
InterVarsity Christian Fellowship/USA, 6400 Schroeder Rd., P.O. Box 7895, Madison, WI 53707-7895,
or visit the IVCF website at www.intervarsity.org.

Scripture quotations, unless otherwise noted, are from The Holy Bible, English Standard Version,
copyright © 2001 by Crossway Bibles, a division of Good News Publishers. Used by permission. All
rights reserved.

While all stories in this book are true, some names and identifying information in this book have been
changed to protect the privacy of the individuals involved.

Cover design by Cindy Kiple
Interior design by Beth Hagenberg
Images: Forest path: © Christine Amat/Trevillion Images

ISBN 978-0-8308-5653-4

Printed in the United States of America ∞

Library of Congress Cataloging-in-Publication Data
A catalog record for this book is available from the Library of Congress.

P	17	16	15	14	13	12	11	10	9	8	7	6	5	4	3	2	1
Y	27	26	25	24	23	22	21	20	19	18	17	16	15	14	13		

To Brighton

*I pray that you grow to see the beauty of the Lord
and be captivated by his grace.
I love you.*

To Kelli

*I pray that the Lord continues to unveil his beauty, grace,
love and glory and lead us in his way. Ours is an
uncommon union, and you are my cherished
partner on this journey of grace.
I love you.*

Contents

Acknowledgments

THIS BOOK HAS BEEN A REAL JOY to write. After four years of academic study on Jonathan Edwards it was truly a blessed time to work on a project that, I trust, honors his memory by focusing on something so close to his heart. There are, of course, many people in my life who have made this project all the more of a blessing. I extend my thanks to my editor, Drew Blankman, for your work and encouragement on this project, and to IVP for buying Biblica just so you could publish my book (I'm kidding, Cindy). Of the many friends who encouraged me and helped me on this project, three in particular stand out. Jamin Goggin, your thoughts, edits and willingness to talk through this process helped me in more ways than you know. Kent Eilers, in your busy schedule you never refuse to read something for me, and your thoughts are always poignant and fruitful. James Merrick, talking through ideas with you has always been incredibly illuminating, and it was no different with this project. I deeply appreciate the friendship that you three provide, and your desire to bridge gaps between the academy and the church. Your friendship is truly a gift from God.

Furthermore, I received incredibly valuable feedback from other friends regarding this project, and their suggestions, insights and critiques helped make this a better and more readable book. For that, I am very grateful. Fred and Linda Wevodau, thank you for taking the time to read the first section and walk me through your thoughts. Your friendship and role in our lives has been such a blessing.

Lindsey Cooper, thank you for taking the time to make detailed comments on an early portion of the work. Thanks go to Kelli's small group as a whole for their friendship and desire to be a part of this process. Josh Weidmann, thank you for reading the first section and for your encouragement. It has been a blessing to get to know you, Molly and the kids, and your friendship has been a real gift in this season.

Last, to my family. My family is full of authors. I appreciate the encouragement from my sister, Alison, a novelist, my brother-in-law, Dan, who writes children books, and my father and mother, who have dabbled in writing a bit. Thank you for your unwavering excitement about what I am doing. Your encouragement never ceases to uplift me. Kelli, thank you so much for the work you put in on my projects, including this one. I make you read some real rubbish. Thank you for reading it, critiquing it and helping me become a better writer. Brighton, thank you for your energy, smile and joy. I hope one day you will read this and be blessed by it. I trust the Lord will continue to guide our family and provide grace in ways we never expect. To him be the glory.

Introduction

ETERNITY SHOULD CAPTURE OUR IMAGINATION. The mundane details of our lives are saturated with divine realities. Our world is dripping with God's presence and calling us to worship him alone (Ps 97:4-6). But our eyes are dim and our understanding is darkened. Eternity is lost in the immediacy of our world. We hardly have patience to wait for someone to make our latte, let alone to set our minds on Christ, who sits at the right hand of God (Col 3:1-2). What does it look like to grasp God's presence and his call for our growth in grace? What does it look like to be God's "fellow workers" (1 Cor 3:9) in the Christian life? What does it mean to proclaim, "Without you I can do nothing" (see Jn 15:5)?

I could have written a book answering these questions myself. But I didn't. Rather, I wrote a book answering these questions from the perspective of Jonathan Edwards. Why? Edwards is considered one of the great spiritual thinkers in Protestant history, and he is often turned to as an ideal example of the Christian life. Not that he was perfect, by any means, but that he practiced what he preached. By listening to Edwards, we are sitting at the feet of our elders rather than grasping onto whatever happens to be new (Acts 17:21).

What follows, therefore, is a journey into wisdom. If you are looking for easy answers or a few simple disciplines guaranteed to bring about spiritual maturity, you are in the wrong place. The journey into wisdom requires time. Wisdom is the result of living out the Christian life—seeking to live for Christ alone. Wisdom comes through learning patience, humility and love. Wisdom entails sitting at the feet of those who have walked with Christ before us. This book is an opportunity to accept that call.

The Road Less Traveled

I am not musical. That is actually an understatement. I am musically oblivious. I love music, but I lack both talent and an ear for musical excellence. When I was in high school one of my closest friends was a guitar player, and I envied that. I really wanted to learn how to play, but I did not have the kind of motivation to *really* learn how to play. In fact, I was fine with just being able to play a few songs. I asked my friend Brandon to teach me how to play guitar. There was a song I really liked and I wanted him to teach me how to play it. "It doesn't really work that way," he explained. "I can't just teach you how to play a song, as if the only thing holding you back from playing Mozart on the piano is memorizing which keys to hit." I just wanted to be able to pick up a guitar and start playing something that actually sounded like music.

This, in many ways, illustrates how people talk about spiritual formation. Many are not concerned to actually understand the depths of spiritual formation, nor are they all that interested in really developing a way of life (as it would have taken for me to learn guitar). Rather, they just want some simple answers to fix their broken lives. When push comes to shove, much that goes by the term *spirituality* is really just an extension of our own desire to have a "better," more fulfilling life. Just as we approach health issues, our posture is about getting it fixed as easily and quickly as possible: *Isn't there just a pill I can take?*

What we are doing in this book can be described as the "road less traveled." I'm not interested in giving you a couple of interesting tidbits to fix your life. I'm not interested in showing you a new spiritual practice or two that might provide some short-term satisfaction of devotion. What *I am* interested in is pointing you to Christ, because that is ultimately what spiritual formation is about. I am interested in turning you to someone like Jonathan Edwards as an example of what the Christian life could look like. Ultimately, the reason this is the road less traveled is that spiritual formation is not simply doing spiritual disciplines. Spiritual formation is about a life oriented to God in Christ by the Spirit. Since spiritual formation is not, ultimately, about us at all, but about God, we must set our minds and hearts on him rather than our problems, our shortcomings or our desire to change. Those who lose their lives for my sake will find them (Mt 16:25), Jesus tells us.

WORDS, WORDS, WORDS

Spiritual formation is the Spirit's work of transforming us into the image of Christ. Some people get caught up with this and other similar terms, such as *spirituality, piety, transformation* and so on. Instead of trying to figure out if we should use these terms, or trying to discern how they are currently being used, let's do something different. Getting into debates about the most appropriate word is a pointless endeavor (2 Tim 2:14). Instead, we will turn to Jonathan Edwards as a source for wisdom about Christian living. In our pursuit, we will seek a distinctively *evangelical* understanding of spiritual formation. What does our grasp of the gospel tell us about the Christian life and faith? Furthermore, if we are evangelicals, then we must recognize that the terms *spirituality, spiritual formation, religion* and *the Christian life* all must mean the same thing for us. We need not grow faint-hearted by how the world and others misconstrue these terms. Rather, we should allow the Spirit to breathe fresh life into them. The key question then is, what do they mean?

Christian spirituality is ultimately about the work of the Spirit to bind us to the Son in love. This is not the "spirituality" of the world. The "Spirit" in *spirituality* denotes the Holy Spirit of God. Spirituality is not about some innate sense of transcendence or something inherent in people. Spirituality is about the very thing we need and do not have—God's own Spirit. Christian spirituality is a partaking in God's work to redeem, reconcile and glorify believers. Rather than being grounded in human potential, Christian spirituality begins with complete dependence, utter neediness and alien righteousness. Rather than us centering ourselves, God pulls us into the orbit of his life, evoking a call to union and communion in Christ by his Spirit. This is why many have chosen to use the term *spiritual formation*, which focuses on the Holy Spirit's work to form us. Spiritual formation is the work of the Holy Spirit of God to form God's people in the image of his Son. Just because the Spirit does the transformation, does not mean we are denied an active role. Quite the opposite is the case, as we will see.

In Edwards's day, the phrase "true religion" was the popular way to talk about authentic Christian devotion. The Protestant spiritual writer Henry Scougal explains this, claiming, "that true religion is a union of the soul with God, a real participation in the divine nature, the very image of God drawn upon the soul. In the apostle's words, it is 'Christ formed in you.'"[1] This is exactly right. Christ formed in us entails the transformation of our whole lives; it means that we take on the contours of God's life revealed in Christ. If the heart is changed, then a changed life will flow out of the heart. If we abide in the vine, we are told, we will bear good fruit (Lk 6:43-45). For the purpose of this book, our focus is on how Christ forms us by his Spirit that we may live a life for his glory.

Introducing Our Guide

You may be wondering why it is worthwhile to read a book about Jonathan Edwards's understanding of the Christian life. First, Jonathan Edwards is considered one of the greatest spiritual thinkers in church history. More important, this spiritual depth was backed up by a deeply spiritual life. Second, as a hugely influential thinker in New England, Edwards's theology and life has helped shape North American evangelicalism. Edwards life and practice has formed our own existence as evangelicals. To understand who we are, it is helpful to learn about the family tree. Third, in Edwards we find a grasp of spiritual formation that tries to balance deep thought with deep passion, human action with God's action, truth with goodness and beauty, and a life of love with the contemplation of divine things. In Edwards's grasp of spiritual formation we find a well-rounded account of following Christ, an account that deserves to be meditated upon in our day as much as in his own.

Edwards lived in the early to mid-eighteenth century (1703–1758) and attended Yale College. He was a pastor for the bulk of his life. Eventually he did mission work among the Native Americans and finished his career as the president of Princeton. Edwards was a world-renowned author in his own day, and his influence has increased ever since (particularly over the last fifty years). Works such as *Religious Affections, Freedom of the Will, A History of the Work of Redemption, Charity and Its Fruits*, and *The Life of David Brainerd* are considered classics, and those only scratch the surface of Edwards's writing. Many have called Edwards "America's greatest theologian" as well as "America's greatest philosopher." But at his core, he was primarily a pastor/shepherd who sought to guide people to Christ. With such an impressive academic resume, a focus on the church and a deeply spiritual life, Edwards can be compared with the greatest spiritual writers in history (Augustine comes to mind). Edwards, in other words, is someone worth listening to.

Unfortunately, many mistakenly believe that Edwards was somewhat obsessed with hellfire and brimstone. Because of this, Edwards is often ignored as a spiritual thinker. Rather, if Edwards did have an obsession, it was the beauty and glory of God. Ultimately, Edwards's grasp of spiritual formation centers on the idea that God is beautiful and glorious, and he calls us to share in that beauty and glory. In Edwards, we find a vision of the Christian life that is deeply spiritual, beautiful and humanizing. It is a vision of losing one's life to find it in Christ. It is a vision of the human heart captivated by God.

This book aims to paint a picture of Edwards's vision of the Christian life and is divided into two major sections. In the first section, I give a broad overview of the journey of faith. In other words, I map out our path. Here, we look at how our path is oriented to heaven, how it is an ascent in God's glory and how it is the way of affection. In the second section, I assess the tools God has given us on this journey, asking what they are for and why we should practice them. Specifically, I highlight spiritual disciplines, what Edwards called means of grace, and then the interconnection of knowledge of God and ourselves. A right knowledge of our tools helps to guide us in how to use them well. Without a firm grasp on the tools given for our journey of faith, our flesh quickly turns this into a journey of worldliness. This second section, which makes up the majority of the book, starts with foundational disciplines (reading/hearing the Word and prayer) and builds upon those to give an account of Christian practice. Not all practices are considered equal; therefore we must understand how these practices are interconnected to guide us on our path to glory. In this sense, Edwards serves as a lived example of Christian faithfulness. Take note at the flow of this book. We refuse to talk about spiritual practices until we have a firm grasp of the big picture of the Christian life. If we started with practices, as so many have, we will ultimately lose sight of their role in leading us to Christ. Inevitably, I fear, a focus on disciplines digresses quickly to self-help. Edwards offers a different way.

PART ONE

A Journey into Beauty

A Journey to See Clearly

Those that are here upon earth are in a strange land;
they are pilgrims and strangers, and are all going hence,
and Heaven is their center where they all tend.

JONATHAN EDWARDS, "MISCELLANIES 429: ASCENSION"

We know that when he appears we shall be like him,
because we shall see him as he is.

1 JOHN 3:2

W̲E̲ ̲T̲A̲L̲K̲ ̲A̲ ̲L̲O̲T̲ ̲A̲B̲O̲U̲T̲ "the journey." Turning to journey imagery was a reaction against the belief that salvation was *primarily* about conversion—a moment of accepting Christ into one's life—rather than about the entirety of life under God. Journey imagery is a biblically fruitful attempt to refocus salvation on presenting our entire lives to God (Ps 5:8; 25:4-5; 27:11). Yet it would be a mistake to assume that this imagery is new. Rather, we have tapped into a deep-rooted tradition in church history. Closest to our own context are the masters of journey imagery—the Puritans. Out of the Puritan movement we receive the spiritual classic *Pilgrim's Progress*. The idea of a pilgrimage to heaven as the framework for grasping spirituality is one of the great emphases of Puritan theology. Likewise, Jonathan Edwards focuses on the image of being a pilgrim in a land that is not truly our home.

This use of journey language raises questions of where we are going and how our destination informs how we travel. The church has historically understood our destination as either heaven or hell. For Edwards, heaven and hell are not merely places, but realities whose powers are *known now*. Heaven and hell are fueled by love and hate respectively. Heaven is a world of love—a realm of beauty where faith, hope and love know their fulfillment in a family of people drawn together to the God of love. God, as Edwards never tires of telling his readers, is a fountain of love. The eternal and infinite love of God quenches the thirst of all who draw near. In drinking deeply from this fountain, love of God and neighbor finally reign perfectly. Hell has no such fountain; it is the natural consequence of a society of selfishness. Rather than remaining on the outskirts of our world, heaven and hell assert themselves in our lives. Those who know God, as revealed in Christ Jesus, have a piece of heaven abiding in them. The Holy Spirit, or God's own love, is given to believers in salvation. The fountain that abides in heaven pours forth through the lives of believers now. Unbelievers, in contrast, will ultimately bear the fruit of the place to which they journey. Those who do not sit and drink at the fountain of love will ultimately have hate abide in their souls. For those who do not know God, selfishness will eventually win out in their hearts; the forces of hell will run rampant in and through them to the world.

Everyone is a pilgrim. Everyone is journeying somewhere. In the fall, humankind set out on a pilgrimage to hell because people lost the Spirit of God communicating the love of God to their hearts. Their hearts, *our* hearts, have collapsed into themselves, pushing our selves to the center of reality (and pushing God to the outskirts or even to nonexistence). Hell exerts its influence through people in the world, forming cultures, societies and families. In Christ, believers are put on a different path altogether. This path is not simply a different mindset. God implants a piece of heaven in his people so that they are brought from death to life. God's own Spirit is given as the Spirit of love, so that the redeemed will live out the way of heaven in the world now. The focus on the present reality of heaven and hell does not, in some way, raise the question of their existence. Far from it. The present realities of love and hate are proof that heaven and hell are real—so real, in fact, that their ways of life bleed into ours.

To journey well in this life, it is important to meditate on the direction your heart is pointing. What realm serves as the true north to which your heart finds its bearings? To live a heavenly life now, one must "set your minds on things that are above, not on things that are on earth" (Col 3:2). The "things that are above" do not primarily reference a place, but the Father, Son and Holy Spirit—the triune God. We must turn our attention to the source of the heavenly life so we can live the "way of heaven" here. To do so, I focus our attention on being with God in glory. Heaven is only heavenly because God is there. He is the spring of love that gives life and direction to that place. The life we know now is still given direction by that same source of life and love. God is the only source of the heavenly life, and therefore to grasp the nature of the Christian life we must grasp what it means to *know* God.

As a child, I loved to go to restaurants so that I could play the games on the back of the children's placemat. Inevitably, one of those games would be a relatively simple maze. Before too long I realized that it was easier to start at the end, to see where I was going, as a way to figure out how best to avoid pitfalls and dead ends along the way. I am doing the same kind of thing in this chapter—outlining what it means to become oriented to the God of heaven, where a believer's journey ends, so that we can live a heavenly life here. To better grasp our present life, in other words, we start at the end—at the perfection of this life in glory. By starting at the end, we paint the journey of the Christian life with broad strokes, which are then fleshed out throughout the rest of the book. This chapter maps the ground we will cover on our journey, and the remaining chapters, in one way or another, offer directions, equipment and sustenance for the pilgrimage set before us.

WHEN WE WILL SEE

The Christian life is not abstracted away from heaven, but is directly connected to it. In fact, our heavenly and earthly lives are not two different journeys, but are two phases of the same pilgrimage. Heaven is not a static realm where we arrive at eternity only to finish learning, loving and, well, *living*. Rather, heaven is the place where God is known *perfectly*, but not fully.

Let me explain. Continuing with the image of God as a fountain, we can see ourselves in heaven as buckets who are full of God. Since we are full, we are perfectly satisfied, but our capacity continues to grow in heaven. We become larger buckets. We continue to learn more about God and love God more and more. As our capacity grows, we remain perfectly full, but since God is infinite he is never fully known. We are always growing and eternally expanding in our desire to know God and love him more—and yet our satisfaction never wanes, but increases exponentially. Heaven is a journey with God where we grow in love and knowledge of him for eternity; where our own love abounds to others in a society of love. Therefore, the term *heaven* refers to the day when love of God and neighbor reign unhindered.

The Great Awakening
1734-5
1740 →
Wesley 1703 *(1729,1730 Same time Eng Am*

When we try to talk about heaven, we run into a problem: there
simply isn't all that much information. Interestingly, in the Western
tradition there is a broad sense of agreement, among both Catholics
and Protestants, that in heaven we will participate in what is called
the "beatific vision." Whether you look to John Calvin, Charles
Hodge, John Owen or Jonathan Edwards, the focus of eternity is on
coming to see God face to face. The word *beatific* is not some
magical or mystical term, but points to the effect of seeing God. A
sight of God, Edwards tells us, is "happifying" (which is what beatific means); it causes happiness to well up inside of the person. It
would be foolish to think that seeing God is uninteresting, or maybe
interesting only in an academic sense. Seeing God fulfills the design
of humanity and therefore sets the mind and heart into motion—it
happifies. Seeing God brings a person to complete satisfaction. Note
Edwards's depiction of this sight of God:

> The Beatifical Vision of God: *that* is the tip of happiness! To
> see a God of infinite glory and majesty face to face, to see him
> as he is, and to know him as we are known; there to be ad-
> mitted into the most intimate acquaintance with him, to be
> embraced as in his arms: this is such a privilege as Moses
> himself could not be admitted to while on earth. The vision
> and fruition of God will be so intimate and clear as to transform
> the soul into the likeness of God: "We shall be like him, for we
> shall see him as he is," says the Apostle (1 John 3:2).[1]

The "tip of happiness," or, we might say, the goal of humanity, is
to see God face to face and be embraced as his own. This is the land
to which we, as believers, journey—a land where God dwells and
where God's love is open to his people in full. There are two questions we want to answer here: First, where do theologians get this
idea? In other words, is this idea biblical? Second, why is this vision
"happifying"? What is it about this vision that causes perfect satis-

faction and joy to well up from within? Only after considering these questions will we turn back to show how this beatific vision shapes the Christian life.

Before answering these questions, let me pause for a moment and explain why these issues matter. We are not told much about life after death, but we are told something. What we are told does not consist of throw away fun facts for playing Bible trivia, but rather is meant to help ground our lives here and orient our hearts to the glory God has set before us. Meditating on the reality of heaven and hell helps us understand our calling in *this* life. This will play a particularly helpful role when we turn our attention to talking about spiritual practices. Grasping the destination set before us helps us to understand the kind of journey we are on.

The beatific vision: Biblical considerations. The biblical material for the beatific vision reads like descriptions of something massive, where each passage reveals a tiny piece of the whole. We have to stand back and look at the whole before we know what we are seeing.[2] Many people turn to passages like Psalm 17:15, "As for me, I shall behold your face in righteousness; when I awake, I shall be satisfied with your likeness," to provide a foundation for more specific New Testament passages. Revelation 22:3-4 is often suggested to paint the picture of the psalmist's satisfaction, "No longer will there be any curse. The throne of God and of the Lamb will be in the city, and his servants will serve him. They will see his face, and his name will be on their foreheads" (NIV). The idea of seeing God is often related to the idea of satisfaction (happiness) in eternity, where God's work of redemption is complete. In this sense, the beatific vision is a way to talk about the completion of God's work of reconciliation—the culmination of what began when Jesus declared, "It is finished" (Jn 19:30).

Life is a pilgrimage of faith that dissolves into sight. That sight is the beatific vision. Since the culmination of faith is sight, faith comes to take on attributes of sight. As pilgrims, we see through a glass darkly, but we see nonetheless (1 Cor 13:12). The life of faith is a life of seeing, even though the "sight" we now have is through a glass darkly. It is by faith, or what we might call spiritual sight (1 Cor 2:14-16). We have, after all, *seen* God in Christ, even though our "sight" is through faith. The life of faith is not void of sight; it is just void of physical sight. The bulk of biblical passages used to talk about the beatific vision speak to this reality—that by faith we taste the preliminary fruit of Christ's redemptive work, and as we do so we are transformed into his image. "Beloved, we are God's children now, and what we will be has not yet appeared; but we know that when he appears we shall be like him, because we shall see him as he is" (1 Jn 3:2). In a real sense, to see God is to become like God. This biblical point will prove incredibly important for Edwards's understanding of the Christian life. Truly seeing God is grasping him as the highest good, truth and beauty. It is having your eyes opened and taking in the reality of who he is. It is receiving the love of God in full and having God as the object of your own love. As Henry Scougal notes, "The worth and excellency of a soul is to be measured by the object of its love."[3] What you love is the true north that orients the compass of your heart. In heaven, God the Father is the true north of every soul, oriented by Christ and set into motion by the Spirit of God.

Building on the insights noted above, Edwards focuses the bulk of his attention on three verses from Paul: 1 Corinthians 13:12, 2 Corinthians 3:18 and 2 Corinthians 4:6. First Corintians 13:12 finishes up Paul's famous exposition on love (which is the subject of Edwards's sermon series *Charity and Its Fruits*) and states, "For now we see in a mirror dimly [or "glass darkly"], but then face to face. Now I know in part; then I shall know fully, even as I have been fully known." The difference between faith and sight is that now, on our pilgrim journey, we see in a mirror dimly, but in glory, we will come face to face with God himself. This, for Paul, is tied directly to knowledge of

God. Knowledge of God is not knowledge of an object, but is a personal knowledge, knowledge only available in a relationship of love. This knowledge begets happiness. In other words, knowing God, as Paul describes here, is always relational. "Seeing God" entails deep relational knowledge that exists in a relationship of love—a relationship available to us only through Christ, the *image* of the invisible God.

The other two passages come from 2 Corinthians. The first, 3:18, is where Paul culminates his discussion of the glory of the "ministry of death," which caused Moses' face to shine: "we all, with unveiled face, beholding the glory of the Lord, are being transformed into the same image from one degree of glory to another. For this comes from the Lord who is the Spirit." Likewise, Paul continues in verse 4:6, "For God, who said, 'Let light shine out of darkness,' has shone in our hearts to give the light of the knowledge of the glory of God in the face of Jesus Christ." Just prior to this, Paul claims that unbelievers are blinded to the gospel: "In their case, the god of this world has blinded the minds of unbelievers, to keep them from seeing the light of the gospel of the glory of Christ, who is the image of God" (2 Cor 4:4).

Several themes come together in these passages that are central to Edwards's spirituality. First, God is known in Christ, his image, and his image proclaims the glory of God. Second, "face to face" is not simply a way to talk about closeness, but describes a certain kind of knowledge—relational knowledge. Knowing the glory of God necessitates knowing Christ, the light of the world, and having darkness cast away. Knowing God entails faith, the "sight" given in this world, and therefore demands that the whole person—one's understanding and will—be turned to God. Third, in Christ we have the true mediator who sees and is seen, and who unveils and reveals. Christ beholds God the Father in the love of the Spirit for eternity, and therefore in Christ this vision is given as gift. God the Father eternally beholds the Son, and as they gaze upon their perfection they commune in the perfect love of the Spirit. Jesus comes as the One who has seen the Father and is beheld by him as his Son. Therefore, in Christ, we come to behold God, because only in Christ do creatures come to know, and *truly see*, their Creator (Jn 14:9).

THE SIGHT THAT HAPPIFIES

Keeping in mind the passages just overviewed, we can now focus on why this sight is "happifying." In short, we can say that the beatific vision is the radically complete knowledge of God and his glory. It is a sight of *who* God is, and who God is *for you*. This sight happifies because it fulfills the purpose of human persons—to know God and love him. It is the culmination of salvation where God pulls his children to himself and communes with them for eternity.

Each of these points needs explanation. It might be helpful to think of knowing other persons in order to understand. Coming to know someone is not simply a matter of understanding what defines a human person. If you were to sit down across a table from someone and ask, "Why don't you tell me about yourself?" only to interrupt them by saying, "Wait, I know you, you are finite, temporal, and material," you would have misunderstood what getting to know *someone* entails. You've confused knowing a person with knowing an object. You may know things *about* someone but still not know *them* in any meaningful sense. Something similar is true with knowing God. Knowing God necessitates God revealing himself to us, just as others have to reveal themselves. We come to know others through what they say and what they do. Likewise, we come to know God in Christ, his image, and in his work of redemption. Both of these are revealed to us in Scripture. This knowledge, of course, is not attained through sheer force, memorizing every aspect of the biblical text in an attempt to know God through one's own effort. Rather, the Spirit of God illumines believers such that

Christ himself, and likewise the Father, are known through the biblical text (1 Cor 2:9-16).

We will come face to face with Christ in heaven. This sight, however, is distinctly different from the sight the apostle John saw that he describes at the beginning of Revelation, from one who is *not* glorified:

> Then I turned to see the voice that was speaking to me, and on turning I saw seven golden lampstands, and in the midst of the lampstands one like a son of man, clothed with a long robe and with a golden sash around his chest. The hairs of his head were white, like white wool, like snow. His eyes were like a flame of fire, his feet were like burnished bronze, refined in a furnace, and his voice was like the roar of many waters. In his right hand he held seven stars, from his mouth came a sharp two-edged sword, and his face was like the sun shining in full strength. (Rev 1:12-16)

John's reaction is most interesting: "When I saw him, I fell at his feet as though dead" (Rev 1:17). John was overcome by his vision of the glorified Christ. A glorified person, on the other hand, will come to see and know Christ and his work not in fear, but in the depths of love. All the mysteries of the ages will be made known in Christ—his work of redemption, his eternal love for them, the mystery of the incarnation and so on. In Christ, all is revealed. Glorified believers will have a mind set free to see and understand. The work of God's redemption will appear "like the clear hemisphere with the sun in the meridian, and there shall never come even one cloud to darken the mind."[4]

Unlike our current depictions of the church's relationship to Christ, which are often stoic—emotionless and without poetic imagination—Edwards refuses to hold back: "the soul shall, as it were, all dissolve in love in the arms of the glorious Son of God and breath itself wholly in ecstasies of divine love into his bosom."[5] People are fully alive in heaven, and being fully alive entails being saturated with love:

> Accordingly the souls of departed saints with Christ in Heaven, shall have Christ as it were unbosomed [fully open] unto them, manifesting those infinite riches of love towards them, that have been there from eternity: and they shall be enabled to express their love to him, in an infinitely better manner than ever they could while in the body. Thus they shall eat and drink abundantly, and swim in the ocean of love, and be eternally swallowed up in the infinitely bright, and infinitely mild and sweet beams of divine love; eternally receiving that light, eternally full of it, and eternally compassed round with it, and everlastingly reflecting it back again to the fountain of it.[6]

It is important to note that the saints themselves do not dissolve into God. This isn't a sort of Eastern mysticism where the ultimate end of a person is dissolving into the being of God. Instead, as the saint comes to know God, and the union between them grows greater and greater for eternity, the saint is upheld and made fully himself or herself. God's purpose is not to overtake us, but to fill us with his life and love. God calls us to partake in the happiness he has known for eternity past and will continue to know for eternity future. Just as God's life is not some kind of static floating, so heaven is not static, but is relationally exuberant. For eternity, the saints will see and know just as they are seen and known (1 Cor 13:12). This eternal journey is a journey into an ever-deepening love. Just as we will receive this love, we will pour forth in love back to God:

> All shall stand about the God of glory, the fountain of love, as it were opening their bosoms to be filled with those effusions of love which are poured forth from thence, as the flowers on the

earth in a pleasant spring day open their bosoms to the sun to be filled with his warmth and light, and to flourish in beauty and fragrancy by his rays. Every saint is as a flower in the garden of God, and holy love is the fragrancy and sweet odor which they all send forth, and with which they fill that paradise. Every saint there is as a note in a concert of music which sweetly harmonizes with every other note, and all together employed wholly in praising God and the Lamb; and so all helping one another to their utmost to express their love of the whole society to the glorious Father and Head of it, and [to pour back] love into the fountain of love, whence they are supplied and filled with love and with glory. And thus they will live and thus they will reign in love, and in that godlike joy which is the blessed fruit of it, such as eye hath not seen, nor ear heard, nor hath ever entered into the heart of any in this world to conceive [cf. 1 Cor 2:9]. And thus they will live and reign forever and ever.[7]

Note the communal and relational reality of heaven. As the saints come to know and be with God, they are bound together in love as well. In heaven, love of God and love of neighbor are known in perfection. Using the image of the sun and its rays, Edwards claims we become like mirrors, shining back the light in full to its source (us individually and corporately). This is why a sight of God happifies. This sight makes humankind fully alive in God. We will be fully embraced by his love and know ourselves as the beloved's own. This, again, is deeply relational and therefore dynamic rather than static. Eternity is ever-increasing and is a reality where we will grow in love and knowledge of God and our fellow saints. There is never any unmet desire because as our potential for more life increases, it is always met with a fullness of love. Heaven is, Edwards proclaimed, a world of love, and God is the fountain by which it is so.

A GIFT OF LOVE

As much as I have highlighted the nature of this sight and how it brings humankind to perfection, I have not focused entirely on the object of the sight. What does it mean to see God? The vision of God is grace, fully manifested, given as a gift of love. Read Edwards's description closely:

> This very manifestation that God will make of himself that will cause the beatifical vision will be an act of love in God. It will be from the exceeding love of God to them that he will give them this vision which will add an immense sweetness to it. . . . They shall see that he is their Father and that they are his children . . . therefore they shall see God as their own God, when they behold this transcendent glory.[8]

Just as the rising sun casts away darkness, and its rays of light illumine those who gaze upon it, so does the light of God's love capture the mind and heart of all who see (Ps 18:28). The beatific vision is God's act to manifest himself to his beloved. Notice again the deeply relational overtones. Seeing God reveals, without a doubt, that he is our Father and we are his children. God is not seen as raw power or essence, but as *my* Father. God's transcendent glory leads to the knowledge that God is *for me*, that I am his and he is mine.

Importantly, we are not left alone to stand before the Father, but come to the Father as Christ's own beloved (Jn 3:29; Rev 19:7). As bride, the church comes to the Father as the Son's own. We are "one flesh" with the one who was crucified, raised and glorified. As one in body, so also one in benefits (as in all marriage unions). So it makes sense that Edwards would say, "The saints shall enjoy God as partaking with Christ *of his* enjoyment of God, for they are united to him and are glorified and made happy in the enjoyment of God as his members."[9] The saints make up the body of Christ, and as such, they come to participate in the enjoyment of Christ's relationship with the Father. Therefore, the saints' access to God the Father is only through the person of Christ: "They being in Christ shall partake of the love God the Father [has] to Christ, and as the Son knows the Father so they shall partake with him in his sight of God, as being as it were parts of him as he is in the bosom of the Father."[10]

In eternity the redeemed will participate in the Father's beholding of the Son and the Son's beholding of the Father. God's love, the Spirit, will bind them to the Father and Son so that they partake in the love that defines God's own life. When God gives his Spirit to his people he does not merely offer forgiveness, but his own self. By giving himself, he gives his own life. The Spirit is the down payment, as it were, of eternal life, where God's life of love will become our own life of love (Eph 1:13-14). Edwards describes this reality in a sermon he gave toward the end of his life. There, he describes this down payment of the Spirit:

> Those that have it [the Spirit], however they may now wander in a wilderness, or be tossed to and fro on a tempestuous ocean, shall certainly arrive in Heaven at last, where this Heavenly spark shall be increased, and perfected, and the souls of the saints, all be transformed into a bright and pure flame, and they shall shine forth as the sun, in the kingdom of their Father.[11]

In the center of this beautiful picture of glory we find Christ, fully God and fully man, with the Father he knew from eternity past and with his people brought into fellowship with the Father for eternity future. The saints come to know God the Father as *our* Father through his Son. Heaven is the culmination of redemption, and God's people will, without barrier, enjoy God fully.

A LIFE LEADING TO HEAVEN

One of the ways Edwards illustrates the Christian life as a journey to heaven is through the idea of learning a song. Spiritual formation,

Edwards tells us, is about learning a song we will sing for eternity.[12] While this image may sound odd, it is one we proclaim every time we sing "Come Thou Fount of Every Blessing." There we sing, "tune my heart to sing Thy grace," and "teach me some melodious sonnet, sung by flaming tongues above." Our call to God is to tune our hearts to the heavenly song of grace so that our lives harmonize with his. This image is a way to tie together the life we live now with the life lived in heaven. The song we learn is the proper response to the God of glory, grace and love. Learning this song is gaining the "taste" of the heavenly life offered in the life of Christ. The richness of this depiction of salvation is not often seen these days. One of Edwards's forebears argues that salvation is "the very foundation of Heaven laid in the soul," that is, the life of God in the soul of man.[13] The depths of the evangelical gospel can be found by wading in *these* waters, even though they are often sold for more shallow depictions of forgiveness. *True religion*, as Edwards termed it, or *spiritual formation* as we have called it, has to do with the divine life given by Christ in his Spirit.

Spiritual formation is about learning the way of heaven (or the "song" of heaven) and coming to *see* reality with one's heart set firmly in the heavenly country. Heaven breaks into this world through followers of Christ who have been given the Spirit, living out the heavenly life in the here and now. That heavenly life breaks into the present through the gift of Christ who reveals the nature of God. Receiving this sight melts the hearts of those with eyes to see. It is not the physical beauty of Christ that melts hearts, but the revelation of God's love for his people through Christ. Conversion, we could say, is finally having "eyes to see and ears to hear" (see Mk 4:9; Mt 13:15-16). It is "having the eyes of your hearts enlightened" (Eph 1:18). Conversion is finally grasping that the divine life is offered in Christ, who was sent by the Father to draw you into the divine life of love.

CONCLUSION

The Christian life starts in conversion with a clear sight of the excellency of Christ and the beauty of God. It is a sight through a glass darkly, but it is still sight. The culmination of that event is standing before the God of love and beholding him as *my* Father, seeing him clearly and growing in knowledge of him for eternity. Most of us currently stand in between these two events. As believers, our lives are lived after this initial sight of the truth and beauty of the gospel and before its climax in glory. These events bracket the Christian life and give it its texture. The Christian life is a journey to see clearly. It is a journey inaugurated with a sight of faith and a journey whose destination is the perfection of that sight. As we look at the Christian life we will continue to come back to this theme. It is the thread that is woven throughout the entirety of Edwards's understanding of spiritual formation.

In 1 John 3:2 we are told that when Christ appears we will be like him, *because* we will see him as he is. One day we will see clearly. The hindrance of our fleshliness will be removed and we will be clothed anew. Until then, we see through a glass darkly. Now, our loves are varied, often grasping for temporal things and confusing them for what is eternal. I remember the first time I drove a car in driver's education. My instructor immediately recognized a major error in my technique. My vision was cast down the front of my hood so I could really only see the road we were just about to drive over. My instructor told me to set my eyes on the horizon, and in doing so I would be able to maintain a straight path. Many drivers, he told me, look instead at the car in front of them, and so they veer to the right or left depending on the tendencies of the driver they are following. "Focus beyond that," he admonished. This book is teaching the same lesson about the spiritual life. Set your mind on Christ so that you won't simply veer to the right or left as you follow whomever is in front of you. Don't simply look down at your feet and miss where this journey with God is going. Grasp the beauty of the God of love, so that the temptations along the side of the road don't seduce you and change your course. "Therefore if you have been raised up with Christ, keep seeking the things above, where Christ is, seated at the right hand of God. Set your mind on the things above, not on the things that are on earth. . . . When Christ, who is our life, is revealed, then you also will be revealed with Him in glory" (Col 3:1-2, 4 NASB).

Mapping the Way of Love

*[Believers] are traveling in the way towards heaven, and gradually
climb the hill till they arrive at the top. . . . [T]he ascent is gradual
towards the top in the way to heaven; the beginning of the
ascent is steepest and most difficult. The higher you
ascend, the easier the ascent becomes.*

Jonathan Edwards, "348. Genesis 9:12–17"

*Set your minds on things that are above, not on things that are on
earth. For you have died, and your life is hidden with Christ in God.*

Colossians 3:2-3

We have seen that heaven is the destination of a Christian's pilgrimage. Heaven is the world of love fueled by the God of love. Knowing where our path leads will help us to map out the path that guides us there. Good hikers don't leave base without knowing the kind of path that lies before them. The nature of the terrain, the undulation and obstacles and the best approach (maybe the *only* approach) are important pieces of information. Knowing these things will unveil how to proceed. Such is true also of the Christian life.

A major failure in spirituality today is that it is seen as an isolated category. It exists on its own apart from theology, church and sometimes even community. For spirituality to be truly Christian, though, it must be integrated with Christian beliefs about who God is. This is particularly true concerning who God is as Father, known in the Son through the illumination of the Holy Spirit. Furthermore, spirituality must be understood in line with a Christian understanding of salvation. This is why different traditions of Christianity (Eastern Orthodox, Catholic and Protestant) end up having very different understandings of the Christian life (and differing understandings within each of them—such as Lutheran, Reformed, Wesleyan and so on). If you start with a Reformed understanding of salvation, with Edwards, that emphasizes *God's* work to redeem and save, your understanding of the Christian life will likely be a story of how that same God sanctifies. Salvation reveals the kind of path we are on. The spiritual life is a part of and a continuation of our salvation. As a spiritual mentor of mine likes to say, we know salvation at the cross. It is at the cross where we find salvation, with nothing to bring or offer but ourselves. It is here where we come to know the gift of God in the sacrifice of Christ as wholly *gift*. But many mistakenly assume that the Christian life is lived elsewhere, as if we get up and leave the cross to live life on our own.[1] For Protestants, the Christian life is lived at the very place where salvation was first known—at the foot of the cross. It is here where we are saved and here where we are grown. The cross is not an event to leave, nor is it a starting line; it is the path itself.

If spiritual formation is an extension of salvation, how do we understand salvation? We have already seen that our union with Christ, known in salvation, will ultimately lead us to the Father. In glory, we will share in the vision the Son has of the Father. We will share Christ's life of love with his Father as we are accepted as the bride of the Son (Rev 19:6-9). If this is the end of the path, what is the beginning?

UNVEILING THE PATH OF LIFE

In our context, we might say that the idea of forgiveness has overtaken our understanding of salvation. It would be wrong, of course, to somehow undermine or question the importance of forgiveness — it is central. But it is not everything. Rather, the broadest picture of redemption is adoption.[2] God is not only looking to forgive people, but to share life with them — to bring them into his family:

> This was the design of Christ, to bring it to pass, that he, and his Father, and his people, might all be united in one . . . that those that the Father has given him, should be brought into the household of God; that he, and his Father, and his people, should be as it were one society, one family; that the church should be as it were admitted into the society of the blessed Trinity.[3]

The images that bubble up to the surface are union, family and society. Added to this is a real participation in God's own life: "We shall in a sort be partakers of his [Christ's] relation to the Father or his communion with him in his Sonship. We shall not only be the sons of God by regeneration but a kind of participation of the Sonship of the eternal Son."[4] We are, in the words of Peter, "partakers of the divine nature" (2 Pet 1:4).

Salvation is much broader than forgiveness. Salvation is about life with God. It is the path of life (Ps 16:11). God sent his Son to draw people into God's life and family. Forgiveness is a step toward a broader purpose, a purpose that calls us to a life *with* God now, not simply to accepting forgiveness and waiting for eternity. If we step back for a minute and try to trace the broad contours of redemption, we see that God descends in the Son to "take on flesh" and truly *be* a creature. By doing so, the Son opens up a pathway in his own life to the Father. The Son, as fully God and fully human, is the mediator between us both. In him we come to know God and in him humanity is sanctified and brought before the Father. As the Son ascends to the Father he sends his Spirit (Jn 14:26; 16:7). The Spirit is given to bind believers to the Son so that we can share in the Son's Sonship. In other words, what Christ has by nature (Sonship), we are given by grace in adoption. We are children of God as we are *in Christ*, the true child of God. By being made children, God calls us to the spiritual life of children—a life lived as a pilgrimage to our true home. This is not a pilgrimage to get away from the world, but to live heavenly lives in it, lives defined by love.

The ascent of humanity. In the Christian spiritual tradition, there has been a continual emphasis on an ascent to God. Themes such as Jacob's ladder and Moses' ascent up Mount Sinai were read in a figurative manner to describe the Christian life.[5] The problem with this interpretation is that it undermines the nature of redemption. We do not ascend to God because Christ has ascended to him in our nature. Again, our understanding of salvation will reveal the path laid before us. For Edwards, in his distinctively Protestant perspective, the path of ascent has already been walked by Jesus. Jesus is Jacob's ladder (Jn 1:51). While our path mirrors his, it is not *our* path.[6] Notice his language: "he came into this world and brought God or divinity down with him to us; and then he ascended to God and carried up humanity or man with him to God. And from heaven he sent down the Holy Spirit, whereby he gives God to man, and hereby he draws them to give up themselves to God."[7] Christ is the human who walks the way of ascent. The ascent of humanity is the ascent of the godman—Christ. He became human and then ascended back to the Father in his humanity, so that God's life would be open to humanity in Christ. The path we are to walk is the path *in Christ*. God does not give us power and then send us off, waiting to see if we can make ourselves more godly. Christ has set before us the way of love. As in all relationships of love, the one we love seems to have a gravitational field that pulls us in. With them we find comfort, satisfaction and elation. In Christ, we find a new center by which our lives orbit in the Spirit. Since the way of heaven has been implanted in our hearts, our hearts are now free to point to God. We now receive his life into our own so we can walk the way of love in the world. To allow Edwards to speak for himself,

> As the new nature is from God, so it tends to God as its center; and as that which tends to its center is not quiet and at rest, till it has got quite to the very center, so the new nature that is in the saints never will it be at rest, till there is a perfect union with God and conformity to him, and so no separation, or alienation, or enmity remaining. The holy nature in the saints tends to the fountain whence it proceeds, and never will be at rest, till the soul is fully brought to that fountain, and all swallowed up in it.[8]

Ascending in Christ is having Christ as the center of our life and existence. It is communing with him in such a manner that we come to be like him, taking on the way of life he lived. Ascending in Christ is becoming one with the human nature Christ sanctified in his life, death, resurrection and ascension to the Father. We are children of the Father *in* the Son. We come to live as his children in the world as we commune with him in Christ—just like the union of a bride and groom on the marriage day that is ever-increasing if they continue in a life of love. "Ascending" in Christ is grasping Christ more fully in love. Ascending is being one with him so that we live his life in the here and now.

At the moment of salvation one is united to Christ. This union is by the Spirit and can never be lost. It is a static reality. Communion, on the other hand, is dynamic.⁹ Our lives, particularly the sin in our lives, can affect communion. *Communion* is a relational term explaining our experience of God. Importantly, even if we do not experience communion with Christ (maybe because of sin), that does not mean that we are not united to Christ. Union is unwavering because of the gratuitous grace of God. Therefore, the path we are on is a path of love as it is a path to heaven. The way is "uphill"—it is a way of ascent—but that is not in reference to "getting to God" or "becoming perfect." Ascension is a way to denote the closeness of our relationship with God in Christ. We are already Christ's. We do not need to ascend to God because Christ already has. As Paul says, "Set your minds on things that are above, not on things that are on earth. *For you have died, and your life is hidden with Christ in God*" (Col 3:2-3). Because Christ is our path, our way of life, we can grasp the nature of this path before us. It is not a path of proving ourselves, because Christ has proven *himself.* It is not a path of building ourselves up so we can boast, because Christ has undermined boasting by offering it all by grace. The path before us is the path of love, and the path of love is the way of glory and beauty. Understanding the Christian life entails understanding our calling as those who glorify God and are made beautiful by God.

THE WAY OF GLORY

One of the great dangers for new believers is having one's language altered without understanding what this new vocabulary means. When we become Christians we step into a new language world. Words like *Trinity, faith, praise, sanctification* and so on, are suddenly presented to us, oftentimes with the assumption that their meaning should be obvious. For many, I suspect, this is also true of the term *glory*. For our purpose, this is particularly troubling. Going back to being hikers on the way of love, if someone ahead of us shouted backward, "Hey, this is really dangerous," then we better be sure we know what the word *dangerous* means. If we mistake it for the word *fun* or *easy*, that sentence changes dramatically. In the same way, understanding the term *glory* helps us understand the realities we face in our life with Christ.

Glory is a reality at the very heart of Christian theology and spirituality. This is particularly true for Reformed Christians, and possibly even more so for Edwards. Glory saturated Edwards's writing and preaching, and here we learn why. Glory outlines the way of the Christian life. Understanding the nature of glory unveils what it means to live *Christianly* in this world. It reveals why we are to live for the glory of God.

Edwards understood glory as a threefold movement. First, at its source, glory is God's inner life of love. As the Father and Son love and delight in one another in the Spirit, the life they know among themselves is the life of glory. This is God's fullness. God's life is infinitely dynamic, three persons partaking in one another and loving each other infinitely. Evangelical theologian Fred Sanders has recently referred to this inner life of God as the "happy land of the Trinity."[10] Second, when God decides to create and relate to his creation, he does so by pouring forth his glory. To refer back to one of Edwards's favorite images, God is a fountain (Jer 2:13). God is the infinite spring who pours himself forth in streams of glory. God communicates a true knowledge and sight of himself in his Son that causes his people to know and love him in return. To do so, God gives himself in his Son that we would "see" him (since the Son is the image of the invisible God). He also gives his Spirit, his own love, that we would love him in return. The third tier of glory, therefore, entails God's people participating in his glorification—knowing God and pouring forth love to him in return. God's glory pulls us into a relationship of love with God.

God's glorification begins as self-glorification. God is glorified in the knowledge and love of himself. This may seem like selfishness, but since God is perfection his focus is himself. Add to this that God is perfect, infinite, eternal and superlative beauty, and it makes sense why God's contemplation is turned inward. In creation, God turns to his creatures, but he does so in such a way as to allow people to participate in his own life. Again, at first glance, we might think this is selfish, but it is not. God's life is perfect love, satisfaction and delight, and so God creates that others might partake of perfect happiness. God gives his own life of love in adoption (Eph 1:5), that we as children might finally know the depth of love. As we come to know and love God, we come to find our happiness, delight and satisfaction in him. God receives his glory back as we rebound his glory to him through our lives (Rom 12:1-2). We function like mirrors that reflect light back to its source.

Using images like mirrors and light to talk about our relationship with God has its limitations and can at times be unhelpful. That said, Edwards and the Christian tradition continually do so. For us, it is necessary to meditate on what those images are *doing*. The danger is that these images tend to be dehumanizing. We become mechanical: receiving light and bouncing it back. In this chapter and the next, we will see why this is not the case. Instead, receiving God's glory and "rebounding" it back to him is actually humanizing; it is the action of God's people receiving knowledge and love and relating to God as a people of worship. Glory is ultimately God's own life of love between the Father and the Son in the Spirit. God's communication of that glory is received as we live in relationship with God the Father, by the Son, in his Holy Spirit of love.

God's glory as life abundant. Focusing on these three tiers of glory reveals that God's glory is relational at every moment. It starts as God's life of three persons bound together in knowledge and love. It pours forth from that life as gospel—as good news—because we are offered participation in this knowledge and love. Last, we are confronted by this gospel as persons who are called into the family of God, called as sons and daughters in the Son of God. As we come to know and love God we reflect God's glory back to him and the world. We become those who proclaim a knowledge of God and a love to God in word and deed. We become those formed for the glory of God.

Salvation occurs at our initial conversion, no doubt, but salvation puts us on a distinct path in Christ calling us to a God-glorifying life. This call is to bear fruit of the kind of life God has, to "be holy, for I am holy" (Lev 11:44), and it puts us on a path we will walk to eternity. Eternity itself is a journey in knowledge and love of God, a journey into deeper and deeper knowledge and love that is ever increasing. That journey begins in salvation and is lived for eternity. Conversion is more than a goal line, or a free ticket to heaven, but is the shape of the Christian life. The entirety of the Christian life is a continual turning to God:

> Conversion is a dying to sin and living to righteousness: but a Christian is so doing as long as he lives, and the whole work, in every step of it, is by the dead's hearing the voice of the Son of God and living. . . . Conversion is putting off the old man and putting on the new man: but the Christian is doing this as long as he lives. . . . Conversion is a crucifying the flesh with the affections and lusts. This also is a-doing as long as the Christian lives. And during the whole conflict that he has with sin, there is as it were an unregenerate part still in a godly man that yet needs to be regenerated. . . . Conversion is an opening the eyes of the blind and causing light to shine out of darkness. And so, in every part of the work of sanctification, Christians, after they are become true Christians, may still complain that they are blind, exceeding blind; they may complain still of gross darkness, darkness that may be felt; and the light God gives 'em from time to time is like the shining of the light out of

darkness when God said, "Let there be light" [Gen 1:3]. And 'tis all an opening the eyes of the blind. . . . Conversion is a turning from sin to God: but the work of sanctification, in the whole progress of it, is a turning from sin to God.[11]

A life of conversion is not lived in distress, as if we need to constantly recommit our lives to God. Rather, the Christian life is an extension of salvation. Conversion is a way to talk about the movement of a person seeking grace in repentance. This movement is the same movement of our hearts to God throughout the Christian life. Conversion is a model of the Christian posture before God: we come as the sinful, blind and those who wander from the fold of God, desperate for a God who gives us grace in abundance, opens our eyes to see his glory and seeks us even in our wandering. Christians continually open to God's grace, rest in his way and seek to have eyes to see and ears to hear. This is a life lived for the glory of God.

Unfortunately, for many, when they hear the phrase "for the glory of God," they subconsciously interpret that to mean "creatures are worthless." This assumption is built on the idea that for God to be glorified humanity must be diminished. This is coupled with an idea, found in many praise and worship songs, that "he must increase, but I must decrease" (Jn 3:30). This is a quote from John the Baptist, a quote that concerns John the Baptist's *specific* ministry in relation to Christ's ministry and has no relation to us. We, as persons, do not decrease for Christ to increase. That is no gospel. Our sin and flesh are not what we are. We increase as Christ increases, because when God is glorified we are fully alive.[12] Because God's life of happiness consists in his knowledge and love, God is glorified as his creation comes to participate in that same happiness. God's self-focus enlarges, so to speak, to pull us into it. As God infinitely loves and delights in himself, so God infinitely loves and delights in his adopted children. From salvation to eternity we are on a path of deepening love, delight and happiness in God. Life in God is not diminished life, but abundant life (Jn 10:10).

This path is not hiked begrudgingly, with a heaviness of step that comes from self-effort. Rather, living for God's glory is also living in his delight.[13] At the outset of this chapter I quoted Edwards on the way of the Christian life as an ascent. But note what Edwards says about this ascent: "the ascent is gradual towards the top in the way to heaven; the beginning of the ascent is steepest and most difficult. The higher you ascend, the easier the ascent becomes."[14] The more one ascends, the easier it becomes. Since *ascent* is a relational term denoting our communion with Christ, we could say that the more we glory in God the happier we become. At first, we are more fleshly than not, but as we commune with God more and more we find it easier to rely on him for everything. This does not mean that we move beyond our sin or our flesh. Actually, the more holy we become the more we are aware of our flesh, sin and limitedness. The more we grow, the more we grasp with all our might the grace offered by God in Christ. The ascent becomes easier, not because we become independent, but because we come to grasp our dependence (and depravity) more fully. Importantly, our happiness and delight will always be mixed this side of glory. Our vision is always through a glass darkly here, and our flesh always limits our happiness. But in heaven, this happiness is let free to enjoy God forever. There, in that place, God's grace draws us to glory in God fully and receive the abundance of happiness only known in a life focused entirely on God.

Therefore, true happiness, just like true righteousness, is always "alien" to us. It is found from without. It is found in another. True happiness, just like salvation, righteousness and forgiveness, is found in Christ. Paul tells us in 1 Corinthians that, "He is the source of your life in Christ Jesus, whom God made our wisdom, our righteousness and sanctification and redemption" (1:30 RSV). God the Father made Christ Jesus our righteousness and sanctification. Therefore, as those things reside *in* him, our salvation depends on life *in* him. In Christ we come to glorify God because we are bound to his life in his Son. This is why the Christian life is the way of love, not only because heaven is the world of love, but because God is the God of love. The Christian life is not an attempt to fix ourselves (self-help) or to seek self-fulfillment (worldly "spirituality"). Rather, in seeking to glorify God in all things, we come to find our *true* happiness, our *true* fulfillment, and we come to know our calling as ambassadors and witnesses.

THE WAY OF BEAUTY

Journeys change those who walk them. The change might be simple: an appreciation for newfound beauty, a recognition of your strengths and weaknesses, or even the realization that a particular path was the wrong one. The journey of faith entails simple changes, but it also demands profound ones as well. As we progress we come to deeper truths about ourselves and God, the path before us and behind us, and we come to glimpse what the rest of the path entails. One of the most profound realities discovered on the journey is that as we travel to the beautiful, we become beautiful ourselves.

Sometimes, no doubt, one's information about the trail ends up being false. Depending on the point of view, a somewhat difficult trail to one person could be an impossible trail to another. But in the journey with God, we do not merely rest on information passed along by our fellow travelers; we also hear from the destination itself (himself!) — God. Our destination is always critiquing, informing and guiding our views about this journey. We have to allow our view of the Christian life to be attacked by God. Therefore, we cannot start with an understanding of love and force God into it, since God is love. Rather, we start with God as love and then evaluate our life and experiences based on the God of love. Likewise, with beauty, we do not start with an understanding of beauty and then seek to force God into it. Instead, we turn to the God who is beautiful to try and grasp the beauty we see and experience around us. Understanding the Christian life entails grasping who God is as beautiful. It is having our sight realigned to beauty as a compass is recalibrated to true north, and as a watch is set to real time. God recalibrates our hearts to the beauty of God. He sets our souls to the time of heaven, so that we can see and distinguish between good and evil, right and wrong, and the way from above versus the way from below (Jas 3:15). God calls us to have the eyes of our hearts enlightened to his beauty (Eph 1:18).

Captivated by beauty. In conversion, the Spirit enters the soul by illuminating the reality of God. This illumination, unlike the flashing of light into a dark room, does not reveal new objects, but provides a real knowledge of them (rather than merely knowing *about* them). An example might help. In present day evangelicalism, salvation is often boiled down to simply believing the right things. Saying the words "Jesus died for my sins" is often taken as a proof of the Spirit's work on one's soul. Edwards thought otherwise. He understood salvation to be more than putting one's theological ducks in a row; for him it entailed a complete change of the soul. The difference, we could say, is between convincing someone that 2+2=4 (a purely rational act) and revealing something as beautiful. The Spirit's work of illumination takes what someone knows and shows it to be beautiful so that the heart of the person is drawn out in love and devotion to the beauty perceived. If the person fails to see beauty as beautiful, no amount of convincing can help. They are, we might say, broken. To see true beauty as beautiful, Jesus as the image of the invisible God, fallen humans need to have their souls altered by the Spirit. Only then can we pray with the psalmist that we may "gaze upon the beauty of the LORD" (Ps 27:4). God's response is to point to Christ.

Think about the most beautiful sight you have ever seen—the

immense presence of a mountain, or maybe the setting sun glimmering off of the ocean. You see it clearly and know you see correctly (in other words, your sight is "true"). But that is not all that is going on. You grasp what you see as beautiful, and in a real sense your heart inclines to it. Some feel a quickening of their heartbeat, and others, maybe a shortness of breath. Deep beauty moves us. Edwards uses this as an example of the Spirit's work in the hearts of people in conversion. He tells us this divine light "assimilates the nature of the divine nature, and changes the soul into an image of the same glory that is beheld."[15] This sight weans us from the world and raises our eyes to heavenly things.[16] This contradicts what many people think about Edwards. Edwards is often touted as a preacher of hellfire seeking to turn people to God through fear. Rather, for Edwards, the fear of God cannot turn someone to God. Only a sight of the beauty of God can save. As Edwards claims, we are not weaned from the world by affliction or through fear, but are only weaned off of the world by the sight of something better.[17] In Christ, God has revealed what is better. Once we see the beauty of Christ our inner clocks are set to the pace of heaven's time.

The destination for the Christian is a sight and experience of God in eternity. It is, ultimately, life with God. God knows and loves himself infinitely, enjoys and delights in his own life fully for eternity, and now calls us into that life. This life is characterized as God's beauty. Beauty, in this sense, is not often what we consider beautiful. Today, when we use the term *beauty*, we generally point to physical things in the world that strike us as attractive. Edwards called this secondary beauty. Physical beauty points beyond itself to a deeper and more foundational kind of beauty—the beauty found in the consent and agreement among spiritual beings. This primary beauty involves one's whole being to be beautiful. For example, two people falling in love is beautiful. The giving over of one another in love, the consenting to be one with each other, is at the heart of beauty.

This is not simply a physical reality. The physical manifestations of love point to a deeper union of two spiritual beings whose wills and affection unite in love. To be one of these people in love you have to be captivated, from the depths of your heart, by the other person. Beauty is primarily a personal and relational reality.

But even the beauty seen in the love of one person to another is not the highest beauty. Even this beauty points beyond itself to something greater and deeper. Rather, God's own life of love and delight is the fountain of beauty, and all other instances of beauty are witnesses to that reality. "God is God, and distinguished from all other beings, and exalted above 'em, chiefly by his divine beauty, which is infinitely diverse from all other beauty."[18] Beauty is not simply another attribute of many for God, but serves as an overarching attribute that describes God's life and being. True beauty, in other words, exists. True beauty is God and his infinitely perfect life of love. It is particular "to God that He has beauty within Himself," whereas our beauty "is in loving others, in loving God, and in the communications of His Spirit."[19] God is the only being who is perfectly beautiful in his own life. Because beauty is a term of relation, all other creatures know beauty only insofar as they are related to God and to others through the love of the Holy Spirit. This points to the deepest aspect of Christian belief, that God is not an isolated monad floating beyond time in a static and lifeless state, but that God is three persons living in eternal love and delight. God is excellent. For a being to be excellent they must exist in love. God, therefore, cannot be a single person, but must be triune. Note Edwards's point: "if God is excellent, there must be a plurality in God; otherwise there can be no consent in Him."[20] *Consent* is Edwards's way to talk about beauty. God's life is a fountain of love because God exists as three persons in one essence — persons infinitely consenting and delighting in love.

Just as in heaven, but now through a glass darkly, we come to see God in conversion and know him as beautiful. Edwards states, "He that sees not the beauty of holiness . . . in effect is ignorant of the whole spiritual world."[21] Or, again,

> he that sees the beauty of holiness, or true moral good, sees the greatest and most important thing in the world. . . . Unless this is seen, nothing is seen, that is worth the seeing: for there is no other true excellency or beauty. Unless this be understood, nothing is understood, that is worthy of the exercise of the noble faculty of understanding. This is the beauty of the Godhead, and the divinity of Divinity (if I may so speak), the good of the Infinite Fountain of Good. . . . He therefore in effect knows nothing, that knows not this: his knowledge is but the shadow of knowledge, or the form of knowledge as the apostle calls it [2 Tim 3:5].[22]

The ascended Son sends the Spirit so the saints can finally see and know, even though their sight and knowledge will remain darkened until glory. Nonetheless, their knowledge is still of a spiritual origin. Their knowledge is beyond deduction and natural formulation, and is only available by God's self-giving. It is impossible to argue someone, or even yourself, into grasping something as beautiful that they see as ugliness (or foolishness, like the cross: 1 Cor 1:23-25). God's giving of the Spirit paves the way for God to be known. Not only is the believer able to see, but they are finally able to love because God's own love has been given to them. Furthermore, God's Spirit resides in the soul to bring harmony out of chaos and bring rest out of restlessness. "It was more especially the Holy Spirit's work to bring the world to its beauty and perfection out of chaos, for the beauty of the world is a communication of God's beauty. The Holy Spirit is the harmony and excellency and beauty of the deity."[23] The Spirit's presence creates beauty. Whereas sin brings in chaos and unrest, the Spirit heals the brokenness of the soul so that true rest and devotion can be known. The Spirit illumines the beauty of God such that everything else slowly begins to dim and darken in the wake of his radiance.

As noted in the last chapter, Edwards grasped onto John's comment in 1 John 3, where John says, "we know that when he appears we shall be like him, because we shall see him as he is" (1 Jn 3:2). Likewise, as we gaze upon the beauty of Christ, known in his Spirit through a glass darkly, we come to take on aspects of God's beauty. Our own beauty is, again, alien to us; it is a participation in God's beauty. While our sight is limited, so is our formation. While salvation entails many things (forgiveness, imputation of righteousness and so on), ultimately, it entails a new relationship. The sinner, cut off from the Father by his wrath now stands before him as child. She who was once rejected before God is now the beloved before him. By standing in a negative relation to God she was not beautiful—she was like a discordant note in a song. In salvation, she is united to the Son by the Holy Spirit and is now in harmony with God and his life of love, delight and glory. Therefore, as God gives himself to his people in redemption, so he opens up his own beauty: "as God delights in his own beauty, he must necessarily delight in the creature's holiness; which is a conformity to, and participation of it, as truly as the brightness of a jewel, held in the sun's beams, is a participation, or derivation of the sun's brightness."[24] God shines forth to his creatures. Those who receive this light receive the Son and the Spirit. By receiving this light, they are made beautiful—they shine with the beauty and glory of God.

CONCLUSION

God is beautiful and glorious in his own life. God does not need anyone else, or anything else for him to be the fountain of glory and beauty. It is out of this abundant life that God overflows to his creation, calling people to share in and partake of his glory and beauty. The beauty of God consists in the life of love and delight he knows as Father, Son and Holy Spirit. Beauty, as a personal reality, highlights the self-giving and receiving, or "consenting," within God's eternal and infinite life of happiness. To know God truly, one must be brought into and experience this life of love and delight. To do so, God gives himself to his creation in Christ and the Spirit. Christ is the image of the invisible God (Col 1:15), the visible image of beauty who reveals that he and the Father are one (Jn 17:11). By being united to Christ, believers have a relationship with God and consent to him in faith. Through faith believers come to be beautiful—to partake of God's own beauty in such a fashion that they become, to some degree, what he is. We consent to Christ by believing in him and loving him. As we grow in faith and love we grow in beauty, acting as witnesses for Christ in the world (Is 62:1-3).

Starting with salvation, and then walking the path through glory and beauty, we have seen that Edwards's understanding of the Christian life is relational "all the way down." Images of glory and beauty can, at times, feel mechanical or feel like they are simply aspects of power—like the sun giving its rays. But these images serve a higher end. Talking about God is talking about God's personal nature. To know *God as glorious*, one must know and love God personally. To know *God as beautiful*, one must know God and love him personally. This kind of knowledge is not knowledge of an object, but is knowledge of a subject. Therefore, being confronted by God is being confronted by the personal God personally. This is particularly important as we move into a discussion of why our knowledge of God must be affectionate knowledge.

3

Walking in Affection

He that has doctrinal knowledge and speculation only, without
affections, never is engaged in the business of religion.

JONATHAN EDWARDS, RELIGIOUS AFFECTIONS

Love one another with brotherly affection.
Outdo one another in showing honor.
Do not be slothful in zeal, be fervent in spirit, serve the Lord.

ROMANS 12:10-11

W HEN I WAS IN JUNIOR HIGH I had an interest in architecture.
In art class our teacher showed us how to draw a building that looked
three-dimensional. His first instruction was to choose two points,
one off each side of the paper, and connect them with an imaginary
line. This line served as our horizon, and the points anchored the
east and west of our drawing. As long as our building lines were
made in reference to these points, our pictures maintained a con-

sistent three-dimensional look. We have been doing something broadly similar. The first horizon point we placed was the chapter on heaven. By focusing on heaven we are able to understand the nature of the path that leads there. Our second horizon point was salvation, and we sketched our horizon line as a path of glory and beauty. When we turn to more practical issues in the next section, we must always make our points in reference to the horizon. The horizon points orient us within God's work of redemption. Third, therefore, to round off this first section, we need to ask how we are supposed to travel. In other words, in light of where we are going and how we are called to get there, what does it mean to walk well? Answering this will close out our overview of Edwards's understanding of the broad story of spiritual formation, which will then allow us to turn our attention to specific aspects of what it means to live the Christian life. To keep with my example, this chapter is oriented by the first two horizons and guides us to discern what kind of building (or path) we are drawing.

To continue the image of journeying, it is necessary to internalize the "truthfulness" of the path you are on. You need to know the path as "true," as leading to your destination, and you need to believe that with all your heart. If, on a hike, you spend the bulk of your energy questioning the path you are on, stopping to look around and see if any other path appears better suited to your goals, you are not going to journey well. In the journey of faith, we must come to grasp the way of Christ. This necessitates faith that the path is the right one. The path for the Christian is one of increasing sight. Our eyes are directed to Christ and his glory and beauty. As we focus our vision on Christ we are reoriented to true north, and all else falls into place around that reality. As we are oriented by true north we need to internalize the truth, beauty and glory of the way of Christ. "Internalizing" this truth is a work of the Spirit, a work we must open our hearts to. This means that we come to trust in the path, or, to follow along with our emphases, we must allow our own ends, agendas and beliefs to be conformed to Christ's. We must grasp the reality that all is for the glory of God (Ps 115:1). We must come to embrace that God is beautiful, and the way he has set before us is a way into beauty.

KNOWING FROM THE HEART

One of the great lies the church is always in danger of accepting is the idea that people are primarily thinking beings. This belief, what we might call the "Stoic heresy," is often ushered into the church through a heavily stripped-down understanding of the "image of God." The image of God is, for many, simply rationality. Therefore, the highest aspect of humanity ends up becoming our ability to think. This is a grave error. Instead, the Bible, with the bulk of the Christian tradition, is concerned to protect itself against the Stoic heresy by emphasizing that people are not simply thinking beings, but loving beings.[1] We are who we are because of what we love. This does not undermine the importance of rationality and thinking Christianly, but this orients the life of the mind around worship. As the quote at the beginning of the chapter denotes, simply knowing the right things is not enough; we are called to love (1 Cor 8:1-3).

Calling people loving beings focuses the Christian life around the heart. All people are worshipers, whether Christian, agnostic, atheist, Buddhist, and so on. To worship is to be human.[2] The gospel calls people to worship in spirit and in truth, to worship according to who God is and what he has done in Christ Jesus. This is not a matter of simply assenting to true things, as if Christianity were a philosophy or ethic. Ultimately, Jesus calls you from your heart so that your heart moves out toward him as the beautiful and glorious king of creation. Along these lines, it is noteworthy that Edwards is perhaps best known in Christian circles for his work *Religious Affections*. It is, in fact, one of the most beloved spiritual classics of the Protestant tradition. In this work, Edwards provides a model of spiritual discernment. The question we need to ask is, What is religious affection? Religious affection is a way to talk about religion from the heart—"true religion" as Edwards would have called it (that or experiential religion).

Religious affection is the movement of the soul in affection to God. It is having your heart inclined to him as beautiful. Religious affection is the human counterpart to God's life of love and delight. To "be holy as I am holy" is to mirror God's life of beauty, glory and affection in your own life. God's goal in redemption is not simply teaching people facts about him (that he is eternal perhaps). God offers his life of love, glory and beauty to people in salvation. Therefore, the path to God must take on those very attributes. God's life is infinite happiness, and therefore God opens his life so that people can truly delight in him. Salvation is a way of the heart and not simply a way of the mind. Salvation entails the whole person, and humans are primarily lovers, not simply thinkers. As God creates for his own glory and portrays his own beauty, he pulls us into this movement of self-glorification so that we come to partake in his glory and beauty. By being united to Christ, God seeks us as he seeks his own glory. Our own happiness and God's self-glorification unite as one, so God seeks our greatest happiness as he seeks his own glory. Likewise, God communicates his beauty to the world most fully in his Son and Spirit and secondarily in the natural beauty of the world. The purpose of this, and therefore all beauty, is to point back to God's drawing of people into his own life. Beauty, in all things, acts to witness to God and his way.

Therefore, to share in the life that God offers, one must undergo a total renovation of the heart. This renovation entails a gift of the Spirit of God. As the Spirit works in the souls of believers, the Spirit illuminates Christ in conversion. Believing in Christ is coming to see his beauty. This illumination is a continual work to "convert" the believer to the ways of God. This is transformation. Furthermore, the Spirit regenerates the heart by breathing his own life into it, and the Spirit unites himself with the person so that he or she may continue in the way of holiness. To correspond with God's self-communication, or, as we have been talking about it here, to walk well on the path that leads to God, one must have an affectionate knowledge of God. But what does that mean?

In sending the Son and Spirit God communicates *himself*. He opens up his own life to his people that we can partake in his life of love and delight. Edwards uses the image of the sun sending forth its light to illustrate this. Note how he adapts that language in the *Religious Affections*: "But the soul of a saint receives light from the Sun of Righteousness, in such a manner, that its nature is changed, and it becomes properly a luminous thing: not only does the sun shine in the saints, but they also become little suns, partaking of the nature of the fountain of their light."[3] We are like "little suns" because we have received God's light. Since we have received that light we have become luminaries (even though the light is always given in grace). This is the first of two images we will look at to explain how we walk the path to glory. The second image is of taste. Edwards compares the believer, who both sees and tastes honey, to an unbeliever, who only sees it. Religious affection is likened to, in some way, tasting.

The light that shines in the darkness. Edwards's image of light helps to explain what religious affections are. God communicates himself by his Son and his Spirit. In the Son, we come to *see* and *know* God. In the Spirit, we have illumination to see and are given the love to respond to God in affection. The Son is the light of God and the Spirit is the heat of that light. Since the whole person must respond to God, there must be a response of understanding and of will, or, as Edwards puts it, there must be light *and* heat: "where there is heat without light, there can be nothing divine or heavenly in that heart; so on the other hand, where there is a kind of light without heat, a head stored with notions and speculations, with a cold and unaffected heart, there can be nothing divine in that light, that knowledge is no true spiritual knowledge of divine things."[4] Knowledge of God is knowledge of a subject, not an object. Equally, knowledge of God is of the beautiful, glorious God. To know God is to love him, and to love him truly is to know him. This is why light demands heat and heat, light. One cannot have true knowledge of God without loving him. Likewise, one cannot have true love without knowing God. Unfortunately, more often than not, fallen people try to have one without the other. To receive *both* light and heat is to understand *and* will God—to turn your face to him in affection.

Edwards focuses on affection because humans are affectionate beings. Every aspect of our lives, in one way or another, is driven by the reality of affection. Affection propels us forward in life. Persons understand and will. As we see our world we engage it in understanding and willing. Sometimes we will things, and other times we will against them. When Edwards talks about religious affections, therefore, he is addressing two things: first, the term *religious* denotes what causes the affections, in this case God; and second, the term *affection* is used in reference to a "lively" movement of the will.[5] Affections are when the will grasps ahold of something vigorously because it is so captivated by it.

When people are confronted by Christ, truly seeing him for who he is, they are affected: their understanding apprehends who he is and their will inclines toward him in love and devotion. At the beginning of the chapter we noted that people are not *primarily* thinkers, but lovers. Being a lover, according to Edwards, includes being a thinker. But being a thinker is not enough. *Thinking* is not the bedrock of the human person. We are most fundamentally lovers. Importantly, Edwards holds these two aspects of the person in unity without them being in tension. Both understanding and will are necessary to truly love God and be faithful to him. But knowledge, without love and affection, ultimately leads nowhere. As we continue to live in affection for God, our souls are conformed to the object of our love—God. Much of Edwards's spirituality entails keeping our eyes on Christ in all things, so that our vision of the world is colored by an affectionate knowledge of Christ.

As an example, I was recently waiting for some friends at an airport that herded every arriving passenger through a single large doorway. Next to me was a mother with her three-year-old son. As I watched the child I saw his face light up. He started bouncing up and down in anticipation, until he could run and leap into the arms of his father—a camouflage-wearing soldier back home to be with his family. The son saw his father and his heart leapt within him. He had waited calmly as strangers and other fathers arrived. But the moment he saw *his* father, love moved him. He had right understanding, it was truly his father, and his will moved in concert with his mind to reach out and grasp the object of his love. In the same way, we come to see God in Christ by faith, and our heart leaps within. We seek to grasp the object of our love.

As lovers, we are governed, in many ways, by our desires. Sin, for instance, is not often an issue of wrong knowledge; it is not acted on because people did not realize it was wrong. Rather, at the very core of a person lies a will that inclines toward the beautiful, and because of the flesh, what one finds "beautiful" is often ugliness. The compass of the heart is calibrated toward distortion and depravity. If we can discover what beauty moves us, we will discover the nature of what and how we worship. The world, with all of its busyness, is moved by the worship of people whose lives of affection drive them. "Take away all love and hatred, all hope and fear, all anger, zeal and affectionate desire," Edwards prods, "and the world would be, in a great measure, motionless and dead."[6] Affection is what makes the world go round. Likewise, affection is what makes religion *true* religion. "True religion is evermore a powerful thing; and the power of it appears, in the first place, in the inward exercises of it in the heart. . . . Hence true religion is called the power of godliness, in distinction from the external appearances of it" (see 2 Tim 3:5).[7] It is easy to see why so many people have clung to Edwards over the past three hundred years. Like the more intellectually minded, Edwards was intently focused on the importance of theology, study and preaching. Equally though, Edwards was a pastor of the heart. He saw no other way to live with God than the way of affection. Therefore Edwards emphasizes discernment, spiritual council and the movements of the heart. Edwards provides a balance not often struck by theologians or practitioners.

This balance between knowledge and will is held together by God's revealing of himself in Son and Spirit, or by "light" and "heat." As believers receive light from God, we become bright. This brightness hits on our previous themes of glory and beauty. Being bright is coming to partake in God's glory and beauty by receiving himself (his light) and by having our heart moved (heat). In so doing, we model the very life of God himself. Recall that God's life is eternal happiness and love. God's life is the affectionate life. Edwards's model of the Christian life is God the Father who, for eternity past, has been gazing upon the beauty of the Son and loving him within the Spirit of love and beauty. To bring us into this life, God gives his image for his creation to behold and his Spirit so that his people can gaze upon the beauty of the Son in the love of the Spirit. Again, this life is had through a "glass darkly"—it is dim, broken and fleshly—but it is still the seed of the heavenly life now.[8] "For undoubtedly, there is much affection in the true saints which is not spiritual: their religious affections are often mixed; all is not from grace, but much from nature."[9]

The life of sin and the flesh dim the light of God's people. It is because of sin that the lives of believers do not shine forth perfectly to the world. Sin can be understood as believing ugliness is beautiful, having affection for fleshliness or worshiping worldliness. In all of these descriptions we see a heart that is divided, a state that will be maintained in the believer until heaven. In heaven believers become "pure flame," Edwards tells us. This idea of pure flame picks up on the light and heat image well. In heaven, there will be no more fleshliness, worldliness and sin to dim the people of God. We will light up like a fire, shining forth the light and heat of glory and beauty back to its source—the God of love who reigns there in his infinite power, glory and delight.

Developing a "taste" of glory. While we journey to glory we should learn to trust the path laid before us. Sometimes, no doubt, we find that the path is of our own making. Our natural affections have turned us off course onto other things we find beautiful. But, broadly speaking, grasping the path of glory is really just grasping onto Jesus. By focusing our attention on Jesus and the "Jesus Way," we come to gain a "taste" for this way over others. Some of the flesh-liness that used to taste so good is now bitter. We are walking a path of putting to death our sin by slowly conforming to God's glory and beauty. In doing so, the sin that still wages war within us begins to die. In Christ, our sight, hearing and taste are now sensitized to a different world, and therefore they help us trust in the way of the Lord.

Many people saw Jesus but did not follow him. What did they not see that the disciples did? Why were the disciples affected by Christ and not so many others? To explain this, Edwards turns to taste. The Spirit of God works within one's heart to give them a divine taste—a taste of the ways of God. It is in this vein that the psalmist would say, "How sweet are your words to my taste, sweeter than honey to my mouth" (Ps 119:103). Without it, people cannot recognize God and his way as beautiful, "no more than a man without the sense of tasting can conceive of the sweet taste of honey, or a man without the sense of hearing can conceive of the melody of a tune, or a man born blind can have a notion of the beauty of the rainbow."[10] The disciples were given a divine taste, and so they sought to satisfy their longing by following Christ.

Edwards offers an illustration of two men, one of whom is born without the sense of taste. The man with the sense of taste loves honey, and he greatly delights in it because of its taste. The other man also loves honey, but, not having the sense of taste, he loves it because of its color and texture. The excellency and sweetness of honey is in its taste, Edwards argues, therefore the man who loves the honey because of its taste builds upon the foundation of honey's true beauty.[11] If you don't "know" the taste of honey, you don't truly "know" honey. Likewise, to know Jesus is to develop a taste for who he is and what he is about. If we return to our hiking analogy, we can say that a "taste" for the destination drives your journey. You hunger for it (Mt 5:6). Others may travel with you who only share your actions, and not your taste for the destination. They have the form but not the power of godliness (2 Tim 3:5). A taste of God is prioritizing God above all else.

For *true* religious affections, the object, God, is primary, and I am secondary. With false affections, the focus reverts to me. The one who seeks Christ alone will know the delight that only he can give. One who goes looking for self-fulfillment will never find it. In other words, having a taste of divine things is what allows the heavenly destination to captivate your heart. Without that taste it is impossible to will God, and therefore it is impossible to actually walk the path to glory. This taste is the taste of heaven and is the taste that calibrates our souls to glory and beauty. This taste creates a hunger for divine things. This taste is not given in its perfection, but is a seed of grace in the soul. Cultivating this taste should lead to a deeper and deeper hunger for God and his glory. The ways of God, the calling of the church, the Word of God and the ordinances of God should all be *tasty* aspects of life. Ultimately, our taste should be oriented by God and his life of love, and therefore the hunger of our flesh should begin to be killed off. In this sense, our taste is similar to the compass whose needle seeks north. We can say that the needle has a taste for north. Around that taste all our other affections should fall into place—the west, east and south of our soul should be oriented by the true north of heaven—God and his life of love.

David, in Psalm 34, proclaimed, "Oh, taste and see that the LORD is good!" (Ps 34:8). In a sense, Edwards's description of religious affection is a call to taste and see that the Lord is good (and continue to do so)! The light of God's beauty and glory is given so that believers can actually see that the Lord is good. But sight alone does not comprehend the depths of the Christian experience. For that, Edwards turns to taste. Tasting and seeing that the Lord is good entails having the whole of one's heart made alive to God in Christ by the Holy Spirit—it is communion with the three-personed God. Tasting and seeing are the kinds of things that beget more tasting and seeing. Tasting and seeing beget desire. It is this desire that turns the Christian more and more fully to her Lord who is beautiful and glorious. It is a journey we will continue for eternity.

CONCLUSION

Affection is the way we travel as pilgrims on *this* path of glory. This follows accordingly since heaven, our final destination, is a world of affection:

> Will any say, that the saints in heaven, in beholding the face of their Father, and the glory of their Redeemer, and contemplating his wonderful works, and particularly his laying down his life for them, *have their hearts nothing moved and affected, by all which they behold or consider?* . . . [T]hat principle of true religion which is in them, is a communication of the religion of heaven; their grace is the dawn of glory; and God fits them for that world by conforming them to it.[12]

Heaven knows the perfection of religion. Heaven serves as the perfect image of what the Christian life should look like here. Our lives *do not* look like that here—nor will they. Edwards's point is not to overwhelm his audience who question if their affection for God is deep enough. Ultimately, Edwards will point to perseverance to counsel troubled parishioners, so that people are not neurotically taking their spiritual temperature every minute or so. Rather, Edwards wants to refocus religion as the religion of the heart. This refocus is on a personal knowledge of the personal God who gives himself to us so that we can be partakers of his divine nature (2 Pet 1:4). The grace given in conversion is the "dawn of glory" to the soul, but, as dawn, it is still dark. We wait for the day when glory will be seen and known in full, but that day is not today. Therefore, instead of focusing solely on intellectual achievement or charismatic excitement, Edwards calls us to focus on religious affection as the Christian way in the world. As quoted above, God fits his people for heaven by conforming them to it.[13] Or, probably better, God fits them for heaven by conforming them to himself. God does so through the affections. The affections we have for God put us in harmony with him (Eph 5:1-2). Being in harmony with God is having one's heart beat with his. It is sharing in the divine life through the Son and in the Spirit and participating in the delight that God knows eternally, even if our experience of it is broken, dimmed and narrow. The affections are Edwards's way to talk about how we as believers become beautiful by being in a personal relationship of love with God.

In this section I have provided a very broad overview of Edwards's theology of the Christian life. As a broad overview, we have missed out on important details, such as: What does it mean to live a life of grace? If God is ultimately the source of my growth (my ability to reflect his glory) then what can I do? What are key aspects of life lived in Christ, ascending in his person to see and know the Father through him? How can I come to see and taste more affectively?

These are the issues we will address below.

First, however, let me recap, in brief, the main thread we have woven throughout the first three chapters. We started by focusing on heaven as a world of love, a place where love reigns because the God of love reigns there. This functions as a horizon point for us, because it helps to orient the Christian life. Heaven is the place we are striving toward, and therefore knowing the destination helps orient us in our pilgrimage. Second, we looked at salvation as grasping both beauty and glory, and ascending to the Father *in* the Son. Jesus becomes human so that we can participate in the divine life. The life of faith, therefore, is a life of grasping the beauty and glory of God and becoming beautiful and glorious creatures of God. Third, we addressed religious affection, which is the way of the heart. God calls his people to love him with their whole hearts and follow him as faithful children. This love is seeing the beauty and glory of God in Christ by the illumination of the Spirit. Therefore, as we will see more fully below, the Christian life is a journey to see clearly. It is a journey that begins with seeing God in Christ through faith. This journey culminates with seeing God the Father in the Son *as we are united to him as bride*. It is seeing the Father as his adopted daughter or son. We see through a glass darkly here, but the Christian life is a subtle cleaning of the glass to see him for who he is, and therefore seeing yourself, life and the world for what they are.

PART TWO

Tools for the Journey

4

Spiritual Disciplines as Means of Grace

Grace must be the immediate work of God, and properly a production of his almighty power on the soul.

<small>JONATHAN EDWARDS, "TREATISE ON GRACE"</small>

Present yourselves to God as those who have been brought from death to life, and your members to God as instruments for righteousness.

<small>ROMANS 6:13</small>

IN THE FIRST SECTION OF THIS BOOK I provided a broad overview of Edwards's understanding of spiritual formation. In this section, I show how the elements of the first three chapters inform a certain kind of life with God. As this section develops I will take a more practical turn, using Edwards's own spiritual life as the main example. To continue with the hiking analogy, this section is where we analyze our equipment. Rather than jumping immediately into practical issues, we must first figure out how our tools work and what they are for. Too many people grab practices from the tradition to "fix" their spiritual lives without ever investigating the purpose of these practices. A great temptation and danger is to turn Christian spiritual formation into a self-help project, but we can curb that mistake by attending to the equipment God has given us to navigate the journey of faith. Once we have done so, we turn to more practical issues of following Jesus. In other words, this section focuses on practical wisdom in the Christian life.

SPIRITUAL DISCIPLINES

"Spiritual disciplines" have been a hot topic for evangelicals over the past several decades. Spiritual discontent reverberated throughout the church, resulting in a growing interest in ancient spiritual practices. Writers and speakers argued that people were taking their spiritual lives for granted and expected God to grow them as long as they showed up at church on Sunday. Like most attempts to renew devotion, there has been much good mixed with much bad. To separate the wheat from the chaff, we must briefly explore the term *spiritual disciplines*.

The term *spiritual discipline* is a well-meaning term put in a very unfortunate way. If we simply play out the natural meaning of the terms *spiritual* and *discipline*, we would come to the popular conclusion that doing spiritual disciplines is how we discipline our spiritual lives. In other words, the term *discipline* makes people think they have the power to form their spiritual life. Rather than being an extension of salvation, we end up with an advanced form of self-help. Just do such-and-such discipline and your life will be better. If you do X, you will stop struggling with Y. There is no doubt why this phrase has become so popular: it addresses our greatest temptation as North American evangelicals. We love believing that we control our fate, and we want the same for our spiritual lives. We want to be self-made people. "Just tell me what to do and I'll make it happen." This is the idolatry of a pragmatic people desiring independence at every turn.

The call to be holy, however, is not the same as a call to do the right thing. *Holiness* is a term that describes God's own life, and therefore the call to be holy is a call to participate in God's life of love. Through this love we are empowered to live out the ways of God. As an example, we could ask how much effort it would take for an apple to become an orange. The problem here is not an issue of effort; it is asking the apple to become what it is not. Likewise, this is a similar question as asking how much effort it takes to make a Christian holy? We can make an effort, no doubt; the primary issue, though, is not one of effort but one of grace.[1] Edwards, with the Puritans, talked about means of grace as the way to understand Christian practice. It is much harder to turn the phrase *means of grace* into a self-help program than it is with *spiritual discipline*. *Means of grace*, furthermore, links Christian practice once again to salvation. Grace, as it is known in salvation, is known throughout the Christian life. Again we find that the Christian life is found at the cross and not a self-help project built away from the cross. Put another way, it is helpful to talk about the *goal* of spiritual disciplines versus means of grace. The goal of spiritual disciplines is often explained as a transformation of character. If you struggle with lust you can find a discipline that will help you stop lusting (possibly fasting, for example). Notice the problem with this. God is totally superfluous to this discussion. You have a problem, and so you come up with ways to fix this problem. Rather than abiding in the vine to bear good fruit, you are figuring it out on your own. Let me suggest that the focus of the Christian life is not about character but about holiness.[2] Holiness is not something you can develop an action plan for. Holiness is not in your power. The means of grace are actions that help us focus more fully on God, recognizing that God is the fountain from which all grace flows. If you want to bear good fruit you don't simply try hard, as if fruit-bearing is an issue of sheer force. Instead, you establish a healthy connection with the tree (Jn 15:4-5). This is more deeply relational than self-willing your life into order. Therefore, while the goal of spiritual disciplines can digress into fixing or growing oneself, the goal of means of grace is abiding in God through Christ.

It is, furthermore, a mistake to assume the modern discussion of spiritual disciplines is new. Rather, our evangelical background has given us ways to talk about spiritual discipline as means of grace. Turning our attention to Edwards specifically, I first outline his understanding of grace. We come to understand how to live in grace by first grasping what grace is. Second, I show how grace guides our understanding of the means of grace. This is an incredibly important issue because much of the modern "spiritual formation" conversation has been reduced to simply doing spiritual practices. I hope it is becoming clear that isolating practices away from one's understanding of salvation is unhelpful, misleading or a failure to practice the Christian life *Christianly*. By focusing on practices alone and their possible efficacy in holiness, we very quickly stop talking about Christ's work to sanctify us and start talking about our own work to grow ourselves.

THE GRACE OF GOD

Earlier I noted that our contemporary evangelical notion of salvation is stunted. The same can be said of our understanding of grace. Again, the issue it not that we are wrong, but our understanding has been stripped down so it fails to address the breadth and depth of the gospel. If the gospel has been boiled down to forgiveness, neglecting the reality that God is calling us into his own life, then our understanding of grace has been narrowed to God's niceness. Grace, as it is commonly used, simply becomes God's free gift of forgiveness. Rather,

God's grace is the free gift *of himself*, and in him we know forgiveness.

As I have emphasized, everything flows forth from our understanding of salvation and the God who saves. The gospel message entails God's self-giving to bring us into his own life. Therefore, the Christian life becomes oriented around the idea of communion with God. When forgiveness becomes the central defining feature of salvation, the Christian life tends to become little more than pretending to act like you know you are forgiven. Rather, when communion becomes the centerpiece of salvation, the Christian life becomes oriented *by*, *around* and *to* the God who communes with us. Our goal is not pretending, but the opposite (as we will see in the next chapter). The "direction" of the Christian life is communion, abiding and resting in God, *so that* we can live according to his way in the world. This understanding of the Christian life has Christ at its center, and his people are held in orbit around him as they live in the Spirit of grace and love.

Edwards, in a depth we rarely experience, understood that grace is God's giving of himself to us in communion. Grace, in this sense, is a counterpart to love. God's eternal life is love, and love will ultimately bind us to that life. But because of our state as fallen creatures, love can only be given as grace. By the Spirit of God we know communion and holiness, and therefore the Spirit of God is the grace of God given to his people. The Spirit of God unites himself to the person and two things take place: the person is united to God the Father in the Son, and the person has holiness and love dwelling within him as the Spirit of God.[3] But these are not really two different things, but two aspects of the *same* thing. The divine "nature" that is given by the Spirit is both communion with God as well as the holiness of God. Edwards argues that, "this is the divine disposition or nature that we are made partakers of (2 Peter 1:4); for our partaking or communion with God consists in the communion or partaking of the Holy Ghost."[4] Therefore, the Spirit does not overtake the person, but the Spirit illumines the beauty of God and shines God's light into the soul. To highlight our earlier emphasis, for a person to have true religious affection, to taste and see that the Lord is good, they must have the Spirit dwelling within them. To respond to God with both light *and* heat, the Spirit is necessary. Without the Spirit people are turned in on themselves and are the center of their reality. By the Spirit, Christ becomes center, and Christ is seen as beautiful and glorious.

The personal reality of grace. Grace is God's movement to open up his life in the Son and the Spirit and to pull us into that life. As a work of the Spirit, grace is inherently personal. Edwards talks about grace as "a companion."[5] Grace "suggests thoughts" to turn our hearts to the beauty and glory of God. The Spirit suggests these thoughts and ideas to us that we may contemplate their truth, just as a "friend conversing with us."[6] Grace, therefore, "is not a silent thing, but it has an inward and secret but yet a very intelligible and plain language whereby it speaks to the person." Likewise, grace "causes inward breathings of soul in the language of prayer and praise."[7] This language of grace is Christ's speaking love into one's soul—a love that causes the language of grace to pour forth from us. One of the movements of the Christian life is to learn the grammar of grace, to come to know and understand how God reveals himself in the souls of his people. Grace is more than God's niceness; it is God's movement of love to reveal himself and draw his people back to him in love.

Grace helps us become dependent upon God so that we can live out the way of holiness. Grace is not ours to have, but resides within us as a person of God—the Holy Spirit. Grace is not some kind of stuff that God gives us so that we can become better people. Grace is not like an energy drink we can use to boost our potential. Rather, grace is a relational aspect of our life with God; it is a part of the overall message of communion and union with God the Father, in

Christ Jesus, through the indwelling Spirit. Therefore, the life of grace will be equally relational. Edwards's point in the quote above narrates this well. Why does the Spirit continue to act in the soul? Not because of anything we do, but only by God's grace and God's covenant with us. In short, we can grow in grace because God has given himself to his people in love and has covenanted with us. We never lay claim on grace. Grace is always a gift. Therefore, in the same way, the life of grace will always be a life of receiving grace from the God who freely gives.

From this short overview on grace we can discern a couple of important points. First, grace highlights that a *personal* God gives *himself* to people in a *personal* way. This gospel emphasizes union and communion, two themes at the heart of an evangelical under-standing of the Christian life and salvation. Second, grace orients the Christian life around beauty, holiness, glory and affection. Each of these themes is a way to talk about the work of the Spirit in the soul of the believer. Grace is given to see and know God, and therefore have one's heart pour forth love back to him. In short, the Spirit recreates God's life of love in the heart of the be-liever. Last, the life of grace is a life of receiving from God what is always a gift. Therefore, continuing our emphasis that the Christian life follows along the contours of salvation, these three points will govern how we view Christian spiritual practice. The "means of grace," accordingly, are God's gifts to receive life from the God who gives in abundance. Turning to the means of grace specifically, we answer the question, What does it mean to posture ourselves as receivers of God's grace?

MEANS OF GRACE

When Edwards explains the means of grace, he uses several biblical images to illustrate his emphases. To help those of us who may not be familiar with the means of grace, I will focus our attention on three of these images. One of his more frequent illustrations comes from John 5, where Jesus heals the disabled man at the pool of Bethesda. If you remember the story, the man remains by the pool because angels stir the water. The first person in the pool after an angel stirs the water will be healed. He tells Jesus he has no one to lower him into the pool, so someone always gets in before him. Most of us, I assume, find this story a bit odd and focus our attention on Jesus' healing of the man rather than the pool itself. Edwards focused on the reality of this pool as a God-given gift of healing. It's important to note that there was nothing about the pool itself that was healing. There was nothing about the act of going into the water that was healing. But God had established this way as the way of healing, and therefore people were called to enter the pool with faith that God would heal.[8] The means given to the church are not efficacious in their own right. God has, in his mercy, given us established means to come to him that we may receive this grace, even though our coming does not bind God to be gracious. Our task is to enter the pool with faith.

Another image illustrating the means of grace is from the wedding where Jesus turns water into wine (Jn 2:1-11). Our role in the Christian life is to "fill the water pots," and Jesus' role is to turn our water into wine. This is similar to my example of the Christian life being the call to turn an apple into an orange. With man this is impossible, but with God all things are possible. The means of grace are ways to fill us with water; they establish in us a posture of receiving from God, and God, in his graciousness, takes that water and turns it into wine for his own use. The means of grace Edwards explains in this example is preaching: "They can be abundant in preaching the word, which, as it comes only from them, is but water, a dead letter, a sapless, tasteless, spiritless thing; but this is what Christ will bless for the supply [of] his church with wine."[9] Without God's direct action on the soul, all preaching will be dead, spiritless speech, but with his grace we receive pure speech from God.

Edwards's third illustration turns to the story of Elijah and his challenge to the prophets of Baal (1 Kings 18). Elijah built an altar to God and put wood on it with an offering. Elijah prayed to God and God descended with fire to consume the offering. In this example, the fire is grace and the wood is our spiritual practice (reading the Bible, praying, meditating and so on). Our actions do not create grace; our actions cannot create holiness, any more than Elijah's placing of wood on an altar *created* fire. Rather, we practice these things out of faithfulness to God, trusting that he will provide the fire.[10] The movement of the means of grace follows Abraham, who had faith that God would provide the sacrifice in place of his son Isaac (Gen 22). In the means of grace we act in obedience, trusting that God will guide.

These images narrate two specific realities Edwards hopes to convey: First, we are called to certain actions—"means"—to receive grace. These actions are powerless in themselves to change our lives or make us holy. If we think they can, the Christian life will inevitably become a self-help project. Rather, we are called to enact them and put our faith in God to do with them what he will. Second, if God chooses, he will endow the means we do in faith with his grace. God does this by his will and grace alone, and it has no direct correlation to the acts we do. Our call, in other words, is not to grow ourselves, but to present ourselves to God through the means he has provided (Rom 6:13). Means of grace are spiritual postures to receive God's grace. To use biblical imagery, our call is not to bear fruit, but to abide in the vine (Jn 15). This does not mean, of course, that these practices are not hard work. Many of them are deeply trying. They are designed to put you into circumstances that run contrary to your brokenness, fleshliness and worldliness. But they do not grow you. If anything, they break open your fleshliness in full so that you are able to hold that before the Lord and seek his grace.

How do the means of grace work? Hopefully one or more of the images above has made clear the major idea behind means of grace. In short, means of grace are opportunities to come to God in a posture of dependence. Means of grace are actions to receive from God; they allow us to drink deeply from the fountain of love. Before turning to look at the specific means of grace, we will focus on how these work. When Edwards talks about keeping our pots "full of water," and, like Elijah, placing our wood on the altar, what is he actually referring to? We must also keep in mind how these actions continue God's work of redemption. How, therefore, do the means of grace help us see the beauty and glory of God and respond in affection? How do the means of grace help us have a "taste" for God's kingdom?

Edwards outlines three ways God uses the means of grace in spiritual transformation. First, the means supply one's mind with correct notions of God and his way. Second, they harness our natural thinking to function in parallel with right notions of God. Third, they move our hearts in parallel with a true knowledge of God.[11] These are ambiguous, so I will walk us through them point by point.

First, the means of grace orient the mind properly to God. To have a saving and growing relationship with God in Christ, you have to know something about God and Christ. Admittedly, our knowledge will never be perfect here, nor does it need to be, but it must have some degree of truth. This explains why so much of Edwards's preaching is theologically heavy. Edwards believed that right knowledge was integral to true growth because it was directly tied up with knowing God. Bare knowledge is never enough. When our knowledge is touched by grace we see God as beautiful, true and glorious. At that moment, we know that the gospel is not only true, but is true *for me*. Take the cross, for instance. When we think about the cross we have all sorts of notions in our minds about what crucifixion is and what it entails. We might be horrified at the notion of crucifixion and yet not be Christians. It does not take grace to be horrified at the notion of crucifixion. But if we recognize the crucifixion as, in a very real sense, *beautiful*, then we have been given grace. It takes a means of grace (preaching, for instance) to set the crucifixion before our eyes and have our hearts pour forth in love. It is only by God's grace that we come to see this act as beautiful and truly grasp it as an act *for me*.

Second, the means of grace help form our minds to the contours of the gospel. This point and the following are linked to affection. For someone to respond to God affectionately—with the heart—both the mind and will must be turned to see God as beautiful and glorious. As we have seen, this entails seeing God in Christ as the glorious One and having our hearts pour out to him in love. Therefore, the means of grace help shape our natural judgments to the judgments of God. Even without grace, people can come to many right judgments concerning God. The key here is that we cannot reason our way into salvation, nor can we reason our way into holiness. Having an affectionate love of God is only available by grace. So we use our natural ability to think about God and the world, and we seek to conform them to the gospel. In doing so, we are trusting that God will take this knowledge and sanctify it for his own glory.

Third, just as we submit our minds to the forming grace of God, so we are to submit our hearts as well. This kind of submission is focused on good and evil. The means of grace orient us to the good of God and against the evil of the world, sin and flesh. Through the means God provides we become acutely aware of our own fleshliness and God's own wrath, judgment and, Lord willing, grace. In this journey of faith, we are pulled in two different directions: we still believe ugliness to be beautiful and fleshliness to be life-giving. The means of grace are avenues for our hearts to proclaim that God's way is the good way. By them we lay open all of the ways our lives reject his goodness. Importantly, we cannot somehow create grace by trying extremely hard to be good. Rather, by recognizing the way of Christ we submit our hearts to God and seek his grace. By faith, in the grace we have in Christ, we come to live the virtuous life—a dependence that bears the fruit of the Spirit.

To illustrate these three points, think about hearing a sermon about the sabbath (a means of grace close to Edwards's heart). Both preaching and sabbath are means of grace. Let's assume, for the sake of this example, that you have never thought about practicing sabbath; it just never occurred to you. The preacher argues through Scripture that all Christians should practice a sabbath, showing how Scripture attributes this practice to an imitation of God. What is your response? Assume that the preacher exposited a correct notion of sabbath and that you have been convinced in your mind and heart that it is right and good. All three components of the means of grace have been achieved, so you (possibly) pray, "Lord, I believe; help my unbelief" (Mk 9:24 NKJV). When you set up a sabbath you do so prayerfully, seeking not to grow yourself, but to be empowered by the grace of God. In this example, it is noteworthy that the means of grace, in this sense, hearing a sermon, ultimately lead us to God (not simply to doing a practice). The goal of the means of grace is receiving true life from God—abiding in Christ so that you bear good fruit. Because preaching led to a new understanding of God and his call, it also led to another means of grace—sabbath. But again, the goal in practicing sabbath is being open to God, not making your life better. Christians do not practice sabbath because we have read recent medical judgments claiming rest is actually beneficial. Rather, we practice sabbath, and other means of grace, because we recognize our need for God. As God tells Moses, "Above all you shall keep my Sabbaths, for this is a sign between me and you throughout your generations, that you may know that I, the LORD, sanctify you" (Ex 31:13). Sabbath is attending to the reality that we do not grow ourselves, but rather, it is the Lord who sanctifies us. As Edwards explains, "attending and using means of grace is no more than a waiting upon God for his grace. . . . '[T]is watching at wisdom's gates, and waiting at the posts of her doors."[12]

Where do the means of grace lead? The means of grace lead us to Christ through the grace of the Holy Spirit. But this is a simple answer to a much broader question. Being led to Christ by the Spirit entails seeing Christ in his glory and beauty and responding to him with affection. It should not surprise us that this is also the purpose of the means of grace. Edwards tells us that "such means are to be desired, as have much of a tendency to move the affections." He lists many of these means as: "Such books, and such a way of preaching the Word, and administration of ordinances, and such a way of worshiping God in prayer, and singing praises, is much to be desired, as has a tendency deeply to affect the hearts of those who attend these means."[13] The means of grace set our minds and hearts on Christ so that the Spirit can illumine our sight of him. The Spirit does not reveal something new. Rather, the objects we "see," Christ in the Gospels for instance, are suddenly recognized as beautiful and glorious. We move from recognizing the truth that Christ died, to internalizing it as a truth for me. It entails moving from the truth that "God so loved the world" to "God so loves me." The means of grace lead us to the well but do not provide the water. They are not for growing ourselves, but for receiving grace. The means of grace are coming to the well and trusting that Christ will give us the water of life and that the water he gives *is* ultimately the Holy Spirit (Jn 7:37-39).

The means of grace lead us to Christ in two different ways. First, Edwards refers to "immanent" acts of grace. These acts of grace do not directly result in a specific practice but focus on the heart. "Such are the exercises of grace," Edwards explains, "which the saints often have in contemplation."[14] Contemplating the divine truth, beauty and goodness warms the heart and inclines it to God, but that does not necessarily direct the believer to a specific action. Contemplation will, no doubt, help form a way of life, but it does so indirectly, as it forms the heart directly. The second way means of grace lead to Christ is through "practical" graces. Edwards offers the example of giving a cup of cold water to a disciple in need. This is a means of grace if you seek to walk in the way of Christ by kneeling before him in submission. This is important: it is not by grace simply because it is a "good" deed. It is following Christ in such a way that the only boasting one has is, "Without you I can do nothing" (see Jn 15:5).

Practicing means of grace does not create grace or holiness in the life of the believer. At best, the means of grace are irrigation channels for the real water of life. Unlike spiritual disciplines, therefore, which often become attempts to make ourselves holy, means of grace demand a posture of receiving. Rather than being in control of our spiritual lives, we come as the needy, thirsty and desperate. Our goal is always God in Christ by his Spirit, and should never be a better life (because he is the source of the abundant life).

What are the means of grace? One way to outline the means of grace is through three broad categories: (1) public means, (2) private means and (3) extraordinary helps.[15] In the first category, "public means," there were three offered: preaching, sacraments, and prayer with thanksgiving and psalms. In the second category, "private means," were listed watchfulness, meditation, the armor of the Christian (Eph 6:11-18), experience, company and family exercise, prayer, and reading. In the third delineation, "extraordinary help," solemn thanksgiving and fasting were suggested. Within each of these means of grace, furthermore, were often several different kinds of practices (for example, under the private practice of prayer there were several different kinds of prayer).

While Edwards never used this threefold way of categorizing the means of grace, it does serve as a helpful framework. He would have, most certainly, accepted each of these categories, and, at times, he did divide the means by public, family and personal.[16] This is helpful because it highlights how a Puritan like Edwards understood his life. The public means of grace is another way to talk about the life of the church, and the family life was, for the Puritans, the church in miniature. These two kinds of "churches" fed and nourished the personal life of each believer, holding them before God and providing a context (a means of grace) for faithful living. Personal life flows back into communal life so there is a mutual enlivening. Although Edwards fails to provide an exhaustive list of the means of grace, he often listed many of them. Included in his explicit lists are things like: Scripture (heard or read), instructions of parents and ministers, baptism, communion,[17] meditation on Scripture, sabbath,[18] family education and order,[19] contemplation of Christian truths, prayer (of various kinds) and the struggle to live ethically (acts of justice, and so on).[20] Added to this are things like fasting, beholding the beauty of nature, "conferencing" (we might call this community), thanksgiving, self-examination, acts of charity and reading spiritual books, a practice Edwards often suggests. Admittedly, as extensive as this list is, it does not cover the full range of the various means of grace, but for our purposes it will do.

Unfortunately, a list like this can simply overwhelm us. When I was in college I read a book on spiritual disciplines with a friend. I recall feeling totally discouraged halfway through the book because I thought I needed to practice these disciplines every day. *No wonder people become monks,* I thought to myself. Rather than seeing disciplines as pointing me to true life, I felt an incredibly heavy burden to carry it all myself. The means of grace, though, are not all created equal. Some are only undertaken in specific circumstances, while others are day-in and day-out rhythms that help order our lives. Therefore, to round out this discussion of means of grace, I highlight two of the most central means: the Word of God and prayer.

Means of grace 1: Word of God. Means of grace are meant to orient us to Jesus so that our hearts pour out in love and affection to him. Therefore the goal of the means of grace is to share God's own mind and will, so that we think and will as Christ does. Just as David is called the man after God's own heart (Acts 13:22), so all believers are called to be "after God's own heart." Notice Edwards's emphasis: "The chief of the means of grace is the Word of God: that standing revelation of the *mind* and *will* of God that he gives the world, and it is as it were the sum of all means."[21] In the Word of God we are given the *mind* and *will* of God for us, so that our own minds and wills can be formed by it (Rom 15:4; 2 Tim 3:16). With the work of the Spirit we become conformed to the contours of the Word of God—bearing fruit according to God's own nature and having our hearts beat in rhythm with his. In doing so, we come to claim that his words are the joy and delight of our hearts (Jer 15:16).

The Word of God is God's revelation to his people. However, the Word of God is not enough; we must have our minds opened to it (Lk 24:44-45). The Word of God, as a means of grace, holds Christ before our view, but not in a way that is efficacious. Without the Spirit, we simply behold a man. Edwards explains: "that notion that there is a Christ, and that Christ is holy and gracious, is conveyed to the mind by the Word of God: but the sense of the excellency of Christ by reason of that holiness and grace, is nevertheless immediately the work of the Holy Spirit."[22] In other words, we can see Christ naturally in the same sense that the Pharisees could. Unfortunately, this did not do them any good. To see Christ as we need to, to see him as the glorious and beautiful Lamb of God, we need the Spirit to reveal him to our hearts directly. This is important for our purposes because reading the Word is often the easiest way to seem spiritual and yet be living from one's flesh. Reading the Bible can derive from a desire to sound spiritual or intelligent. Reading the Bible can be fueled by guilt and a desire to rid oneself of guilt. It can, furthermore, be a fleshly attempt to earn God's favor. The end of the flesh is always self, but the end of grace is God. It can be easy to know the Bible and fail to know Jesus. To truly *know* God and his Word is to read the Bible with a posture of receiving from the Spirit.

As God's primary means of revealing himself in Christ Jesus, the Bible serves to orient all of the other means of grace. This is why it is primary. "God uses all manner of means with us; he speaks to us not only by his word, but by sensible figures and representations of spiritual things [for example, baptism and Lord's Supper]."[23] To understand how baptism and the Lord's Supper represent God's way and truth, we have to know Scripture. To grasp how the beauty of creation images God's own beauty, we have to know Scripture. To understand how to lead our families, to pray, to fast, to meditate upon and contemplate God's truth, we have to know the Scriptures. That said, by knowing the Word, we hear God speak through baptism, the Lord's Supper and nature. We hear his voice in his creation because he speaks to us through his Spirit in his acts. But we can only hear this if we know his written Word. Hearing and reading the Word of God is the bedrock upon which we faithfully practice the means of grace, because hearing and reading the Word are grounded in Christ. It is here, in the Word that reveals Christ, where all other means of grace are understood.

Edwards calls the Word of God the "chief" and "soul" of the means of grace. More than anything else, it serves to center our practice of the faith. In the Word of God we learn heaven's language, so that when we interact with others, gaze upon creation's beauty, pray, fast, keep sabbath, meditate and contemplate the truths of God, we come to "hear" and "read" about God's truthfulness and faithfulness everywhere we look. No wonder Edwards could say, "I am not ashamed to own that I believe that the whole universe, heaven and earth, air and seas, and the divine constitution and history of the holy Scriptures, [to] be full of images of divine things, as full as a language is of words."[24] The Scriptures are the musical score that teaches the song of God, and all creation serves as the symphony proclaiming the glory and beauty of its Creator. As we "read" all reality, we bask in the glory, beauty and goodness of the God of grace. Our hearts are moved in love as we both watch and participate in the "theatre of God's glory."

Means of grace 2: Prayer. If the Word of God is meant to orient the means of grace appropriately, then prayer gives them life. These two means of grace must go hand in hand: "Conversation between God and mankind in this world is maintained by God's word on his part, and prayer on ours. By the former he speaks to us and expresses his mind to us; by the latter we speak to him and express our minds to him."[25] Since the Word of God is foundational to practicing the means of grace, so prayer is foundational, because prayer is our counterpart to God's Word. Therefore, to close out our chapter on means of grace, we look at three aspects of prayer, focusing first on prayer as a means of grace, second on the formative power of prayer and third on the personal dimension of prayer.

- *Prayer as a means of grace.* Prayer is our second foundation for the means of grace. Edwards tells us, "That which is necessary in prayer is necessary in faith; for prayer is only the particular exercise and expression of our faith before God."[26] Or, in other words, we could say that those with faith are those that pray—that prayer is the "voice of faith," as Edwards claims.[27] As one scholar summarizes Edwards's view: "the church has only one posture: prayer."[28] Even when engaging the Word of God, one must be in prayer. God's Word is not simply an information download to make sure God's people have the right beliefs about things; it is ultimately aimed at orienting the believer to Christ in love. This does not diminish the fact that God's Word is meant to guide us and form our thoughts, but this focus on truth needs to be balanced by the good and the beautiful. Truth is not an isolated virtue in the Christian life because truth is ultimately about God. Truth needs to be understood in the sphere of relationships. To know God truly, one must come before God as he is presented to us in Scripture in the posture of prayer.

Prayer can be practiced from the flesh, but it is probably the least-used means of grace to try to better ourselves. Prayer does not provide the same sense of accomplishment as reading the Bible, going to church or even fasting. Edwards notes that many people leave off praying in secret because they can do so without anyone noticing (and it puffs up less than praying in public, Mt 6:5-6).[29] Prayer is often difficult and comes with little obvious *natural* reward. Even though prayer seems clearly focused on God, it is often focused on anything *but* God. Prayer is easily filled with attempts to lure God to our side or leverage God's help to secure the kind of life we want (contra to Gethsemane, Mt 26:39). Rather, prayer is about seeking God himself.[30] *He is the good* we seek in prayer, not the possible response he will give. Like all of the means of grace, our response to God is to seek him and not his benefits. In this sense, prayer must be by faith (Jas 5:15). Faith is the only way to orient our minds and hearts to God in Christ—to truly *see* him. Depending on God can only be accomplished by faith; all other attempts are self-reliance hiding under a Christian-looking cloak.

> He that don't pray in faith, don't look to God in his prayer; he looks somewhere else. He directs his words to God, but at the same time looks, it may be, to himself . . . or looks to nothing at all. He prays with that unbelief and discouragement that he has no dependence on God, his mercy, or any other of his perfections for the bestowment of the blessings he asks. And so the heart directs no prayer to God, whatever the mouth utters. There is no other way that the heart can look to God,

but only looking by faith, by faith seeking the blessing of God,
and by faith depending on God for the mercy sought.[31]

Since we are called to know God from our hearts, we must pray
from our hearts. Prayer from the heart is the prayer of faith, and
all else is faithless talking at God. Prayer is the voice of faith; it is
the Spirit of God breathing through the person to converse with
God. Edwards tell us, "The true spirit of prayer is no other than
God's own Spirit dwelling in the hearts of the saints. And as this
spirit comes from God, so doth it naturally tend to God in holy
breathings and pantings. It naturally leads to God, to converse
with him by prayer."[32] This encompasses the posture of prayer: a
longing to commune with God. As such, it is the Spirit that orients
our hearts to true north. In other words, in prayer, we set our
minds on heaven: believers "have an intercourse with heaven by
meditation, and prayer, and other duties of religion. They with a
spiritual eye do see Christ, and have access to him to converse;
and Christ by his spirit communicates himself to them, so that
there is a spiritual converse between them and Christ Jesus."[33] In
prayer, we come to see and converse with Christ by faith because
we have been given the Spirit of prayer to dwell within us, a Spirit
that "groans" with longings too deep for words (Rom 8:26). It is
this Spirit that "searches everything, even the depths of God"
(1 Cor 2:10), and it is this Spirit who searches and knows us as well.

In short, prayer brings us before God and sets our minds and
hearts upon him. The prayer of faith is a means of grace because
it leads us before God as he really is, creating the space to be with
him as we really are. In the prayer of faith we come needy, dependent and longing for his grace. Ultimately, the prayer of faith
longs for God and God alone. Without it, Edwards suggests, the
Christian life is vain and lacks meaning.[34]

- *The formative power of prayer.* True prayer is oriented to God and not to ourselves and our needs. That said, it would be foolish to neglect the formative power of prayer. As we turn to God in prayer, God bestows his grace upon us to recalibrate our hearts to him as our true north. The effect in our hearts is a "sensible acknowledgement of our dependence upon him to his glory."[35] Again we see God's glory taking center stage. We are made alive when we partake in God's glory, and therefore we pray as an overflow of that new life in him. Prayer is a posture of dependence; through it, he forms us to receive him into our lives.[36] As we receive grace from God we are formed into "receivers" of his love, beauty, grace and glory. We are formed to be receivers of himself, or, to utilize Jesus' imagery, we are branches that have been engrafted in the vine (Jn 15:1-5). Every spiritual posture takes the form of prayer.

God makes his followers receivers of his grace by forming them according to who he is and who they are. A true understanding of who God is necessarily recognizes God as the author of all.[37] True knowledge entails laying down our own understanding of the way the world works and turning to trust in God. Edwards compares this with a poor man who is lost and unwilling to follow a guide. "He must consider that he is lost and knows not where he is," and he "must not follow his own notion but must follow the direction of one who knows."[38] Therefore, for those who struggle in prayer, who find themselves alone, confused, frustrated and ready to give up, he says, "You must follow your guide, which is the Word of God, which directs you still to pray and to seek and follow on."[39] The goal of prayer is not to feel complete, satisfied or elated, but to come before God and seek him as he is. Prayer, ultimately, is the posture of the means of grace. This posture of receiving from God highlights the importance of knowing God and knowing ourselves truly—that we may undermine our tendency to self-deception. Knowing who God is and who we are helps us understand what the posture of prayer truly is. Note the italics:

It may be when you have seemed to pray, and though you
have prayed often and very earnestly, yet it has been far
from being done with a *meek, humble* sense of the holy
sovereignty of God; and how you *depended* on God, and
deserved not the mercy sought; and how that God, not-
withstanding anything of you, even might justly deny the
benefit. Christ so came like a humble, meek suppliant to
the throne of grace with a *quiet, calm, humble, waiting,
hoping* disposition. It may be, on the contrary, your peti-
tions were put up with an inwardly *unquiet, turbulent, discontented, unsubmissive* sort of spirit. A prayer that is put
up after this manner, is no real prayer. Such persons don't
act the part of beggars that supplicate and pray, but of cred-
itors that demand their dues.[40]

Those who have a meek and humble disposition are depending
upon God and will have hearts that are quiet, calm, humble,
waiting and hoping. In contrast is the heart that is turbulent, unquiet, discontented and so on. This is helpful to note because it
colors Edwards's view of the ideal Christian existence. People of
prayer are re-collected, we might say, around who they are in
Christ. They are at rest in him. Their hearts are not tossed "to and
fro by the waves" (Eph 4:14) but are grounded in Christ and de-
tached from worldly things. Ultimately, these people are oriented
by God's glory so that they are free to be fully alive as those who
radiate his glory back to him.

- *The personal dimension of prayer*. As a means of grace, prayer is
  oriented to God in Christ by the Spirit and is deeply formative
  when God offers his grace. Prayer, furthermore, is for the glory
  of God, so that prayer and the abundant life go hand in hand.
  Prayer is not something that wanes when life is going well.
  Rather, for the Christian, prayer is the way of life—the way of

faith—such that Edwards can say, "Faith in God is expressed in praying to God."[41] As such, prayer is the result of faith in a personal God. I have shown how concepts like glory and beauty, which can be thought to be impersonal, are actually deeply personal. Likewise, prayer is not simply an exercise in devotion, but is a central relational component to knowing God. Prayer is important because the Christian life is about personally relating to a personal God.

Therefore, in light of the personal nature of prayer, and our emphasis on knowing God as he is and ourselves as we are, we must pray from our hearts. People "oftentimes pray to God in their words," Edwards tells us, "when there is no such thing as prayer in the heart."[42] Furthermore, "because their prayer is not the voice of the heart, but only of the mouth," so it is "the prayer only of the body, and not the soul."[43] The mistake is not coming to God as you really are. One attempts to placate God by turning the means of grace into a magic trick for growth. This kind of prayer is not fueled by the glory of God, the beauty of God or communion with God, but is driven by selfishness. Praying in this manner is trying to get God to bless you by offering him superficial devotion. This kind of prayer is an act of foolishness. Edwards, by contrast, devoted himself to pray from the depths of his heart. In his diary he admonished himself:

> As a help against that inward shameful hypocrisy, to confess frankly to myself all that which I find in myself, either infirmity or sin; also to confess to God, and open the whole case to him . . . and humbly and earnestly implore of him the help that is needed; not in the least to endeavor to smother over what is in my heart, but to bring it all out to God and my conscience. By this means, I may arrive at greater knowledge of my own heart.[44]

Edwards's goal was not self-knowledge for its own sake but self-knowledge for the purpose of opening fully to God. This knowledge is for a deep and abiding relationship with God. This relationship demands honesty, humility and love. Edwards, like most Puritans, turned to the image of marriage to explain Christ's relationship with the church. In this sense, communication is paramount to a healthy relationship. Prayer is our response to a God who has redeemed us and has offered up himself to us in Christ. Prayer is the reaction to a God who is not silent, but reveals himself to the world and gives us his Word. Ultimately, prayer "is the way to a life of communion with God."[45]

CONCLUSION

Grace is primarily about God opening up his life to us in his Son and pulling us into that life by the Spirit. This movement inaugurates the abundant life, a life lived through the power and presence of God. This life is light—light received from God and rebounded back to him and the world. This life is a life of grace, beauty and love, where love of God and neighbor are united in a singular path one walks with God. This life, Edwards continually reminds us, revolves around glorifying God. Spiritual formation, therefore, is being formed for the glory of God, that his way is known and walked in this world.

To live this life, the followers of Christ orient their lives around his presence and power. This orientation, what I have called a recalibration of our hearts around God, is sought through the means of grace. Recalibration is not achieved *by* the means of grace, but they create space in our lives to turn to God in dependence and seek his grace. As such, our calling is to present ourselves as those open to the Lord and his work, trusting that "there is therefore now no condemnation for those who are in Christ Jesus" (Rom 8:1), and that "for those who love God all things work together for good" (Rom 8:28). Our calling is to abide in the vine, to seek God through his Word and in prayer, not as a way to lure God to our aid, but to seek him as he really is in light of who we really are. Therefore, instead of using the term *spiritual disciplines*, which points to a stance of independence and self-help, it would be better to use the term *spiritual postures*. These means of grace are ways to posture ourselves in the Spirit to God in Christ. Our "discipline" is really just a posturing. As we have seen, our posture in the Spirit is one of receiving. In light of this theme, we look now at how the knowledge of God and knowledge of ourselves shape life with God.

5

Knowledge of God and Knowledge of Self

'Tis one thing wherein man differs from the brute creatures, that he is capable of self reflection—of reflecting upon his own actions and what passes in his own mind and considering the nature and quality thereof, and doubtless it was partly for this end that God gave us this power that is denied other creatures, that we might know ourselves and consider our own ways.

JONATHAN EDWARDS,
"SERMON ON PS. 139:23-24 (SEPTEMBER 1733)"

For I delight in the law of God, in my inner being, but I see in my members another law waging war against the law of my mind and making me captive to the law of sin that dwells in my members.

ROMANS 7:22-23

Dᴜʀɪɴɢ ᴍʏ sᴇᴍɪɴᴀʀʏ ᴅᴀʏs I ᴏғᴛᴇɴ inhabited local coffee shops to saturate myself with enough caffeine and coffee aroma to keep my attention span at full volume. On one such occasion, I peered over the mountain of books on my table and noticed a man staring in my direction. He was on a rest break from working construction outside with several of his crew and failed to hide his curiosity about my work. While waiting in a small crowd for his drink, he meandered into my territory and sat down across from my book fortress. After some initial questions about what I was studying and why, he went on to tell me that he was a Christian who had a continual struggle with a heroin addiction. Interestingly enough, this revelation is not what stands out in my memory. Instead, it is what he said next. Even though he told me about his heroin addiction in a normal conversational voice—plenty loud to be heard by others— he decided his next statement needed a bit more privacy. He leaned in close as if he was worried someone might hear, and he quietly asked, "I've heard there are some people who study theology and it doesn't change their lives. Is *that* true?" It was as though he were asking me about unicorns or being abducted by aliens. *Could something this absurd actually happen?* asked the Christian man with the heroin addiction.

We see two very different Christian people in this story. Both people know God, to some degree, and yet both are so unaware of themselves that their own sin seems innocuous. Both have become so used to certain sins that they are no longer potent and devastating. They each, in their own ways, fail to truly know themselves. I was interacting with someone addicted to heroin, which was, as far as I know, a first for me. If someone would have inquired just prior if I thought a Christian *could* be addicted to heroin, I would have had to think long and hard about it. My gut-inclination would have been no, because it is always easier to judge others' sins as worse than your

own (Mt 7:1-5). In an interesting reversal, this man asked about a sin
that was as absurd to him as heroin was to me, but now I found
myself on the other side. I have known and seen the reality of
studying Scripture, theology and ministry without having Christ at
the center. I have experienced *that* absurdity. Here, therefore, we
look at how knowledge of God and knowledge of ourselves are inter-
twined, and introduce another foundational spiritual posture of the
Christian life—self-examination.

KNOWING GOD DEMANDS KNOWING SELF

To know God we have to know ourselves, because knowing God entails coming into relationship with him. If God were simply an object,
we could know "it" without knowing ourselves. Knowing an object
does not call us into relationship. But to know God, actually know
him personally rather than simply know *about* him, we stand in a relationship of judgment and redemption. God is not truly known by
those he is not in relationship with. Satan's knowledge of God is true,
we are told (Jas 2:19), but it is knowledge *about* God rather than a real
abiding knowledge *of* God. A real knowledge of God is knowledge
abiding in love—an affectionate knowledge that God is beautiful and
glorious. Everything we know about God, in other words, helps
define who we are, because *who* we are is ultimately known in relation to who God is and what God has called us to.

John Calvin starts his *Institutes of the Christian Religion* by
saying, "Nearly all the wisdom we possess, that is to say, true and
sound wisdom, consists of two parts: the knowledge of God and of
ourselves."[1] Calvin goes on to expand on this idea by claiming, "it is
certain that man never achieves a clear knowledge of himself unless
he has first looked upon God's face, and then descends from contemplating him to scrutinizing himself."[2] Edwards advanced his
thinking within this tradition, which helped form his own understanding of knowing God. To know God truly you must descend

into yourself with true self-knowledge, knowing who it is who has been redeemed.

Self-knowledge is necessary for knowing God because the knowledge of God calls *us* into account. When people are not open to self-knowledge, they either become hypocrites or are naively deceived (1 Jn 1:8-10). The self-knowledge Edwards is concerned about is twofold: first, it concerns who we are as creatures before our Creator, and second, it grasps our own sinful hearts before a holy God.[3] In this first instance, he would say, "For he that loves God will be disposed to acknowledge the distance there is between God and him."[4] The more one knows God the more aware she is of the complete and utter dependence she must have upon him. To go back to our first chapter, this means that for eternity we are growing in the realization that we need God for everything, and yet in that neediness we are fully and abundantly satisfied in all he provides. The emphasis here is that we, as creatures, even prior to the fall, are infinitesimal before the infinite God of glory. In the second instance, knowing the reality of our sinful hearts, Edwards admonishes, "We ought diligently to consider why it is that we pray and read and hear and sing Psalms, whether out of love of reputation and fear of disgrace; or whether only from custom, education, and fashion; or whether we do it from love to God and godliness."[5] This second instance concerns the reality of our sin before a holy God and demands that we meditate upon the reality of that sinfulness. Self-knowledge necessitates a deep knowledge of your heart, because knowing God is not simply knowing about God, but knowing him relationally. It means knowing God affectionately, knowing him in love. He tells us that we need to know about our heart's inward motions and passions, and that we should meditate on what drives us. This, we should note, is not simply about what drives us to sin, but what drives us to pray, read, hear and sing psalms (and all Christian practices).

Only knowing God as Creator reveals who we are as creatures. Only knowing God as sovereign Lord unveils that we are lowly. Only by knowing the work of Christ on the cross do we grasp our dependence upon him for everything. In the midst of that dependence we are called to unveil our hearts before God, to cry out with the psalmist, "Search me, O God, and know my heart! Try me and know my thoughts!" (Ps 139:23). Only in the grace of God can we open the depths of our depravity before him. Unfortunately, many people try to live in the grace of God and project a false self to him (Ps 32:3-4). Many try to know God without allowing that knowledge to penetrate to the depths of their hearts. Rather, our call is to have a healthy self-awareness so we can hold open our failures to God: how we praise him with our mouths only, pray to him out of guilt and use relationships to build ourselves up rather than glorify Christ. Without the self-awareness to unveil how much of our Christian practice is built on our flesh, we inevitably fail to recognize how our "virtues" are simply vices in disguise.

In light of this, Edwards warns against trusting too quickly in your own humility and experience. False humility, he explains, often leads people to reflect on the greatness of their humility, just like false love leads people to be in awe of the greatness of their love. "The very food and nourishment of false experience, is to view itself, and take much notice of itself; and its very breath and life is to talk much of itself, or some way to be showing itself."[6] True humility and true love have a different foundation than this, and the path they take is guided by different directions. True humility, for instance, leads to a focus on Christ and his glory rather than oneself. Therefore, to be humble, to know God and know yourself truly, you must grasp God's beauty and your own ugliness. "The light of God's beauty, and that alone, truly shows the soul its own deformity, and effectually inclines it to exalt God, and abase itself."[7] Coming to taste true humility makes pride bitter and rotten. A focus on God leads us, as Calvin stated, to turn toward ourselves. That movement is not to self-centeredness, but is a turn to God as you really are.

For many, I assume, this idea carries with it a sense of fear. The degree to which we are afraid of revealing our sin to God is the degree to which we are still trying to save ourselves. Instead of making us overwhelmed and faint-hearted, these discoveries of sin provide us with opportunities to relish in God's grace. Revelation of sin is an opportunity to throw ourselves on him and him alone. "For you did not receive the spirit of slavery to fall back into fear, but you have received the Spirit of adoption as sons, by whom we cry, 'Abba! Father!'" (Rom 8:15). We seek a true knowledge of ourselves so we can turn our hearts more fully to God, because the truth of sin in us is not the entire truth—we are adopted children of God! Without the knowledge that we still live according to the flesh under the guise of "Christian" living, many continue to worship God in their flesh, let their pride run their ministries and allow guilt to be the dominating influence in their hearts.

Imitation of Christ. In the shadow of God's glory we grasp our sinfulness, and in gazing upon his beauty we see the ugliness of our deformity. Edwards states, "he that has much grace, apprehends much more than others, that great height to which his love ought to ascend; and he sees better than others, how little a way he has risen towards that height."[8] Grace leads to a recognition of the infinite distance between God and us. In grace we grow more and more in awe of God's saving work. God's work does not seem less amazing; rather, it appears even more amazing and necessary as we grow in grace. Therefore, the knowledge of who we are in light of who God is leads to the virtue of humility. Humility, which builds on the interdependence of knowledge of God and self, depends on an imitation of Christ. Christ is our example of knowledge and humility:

> So the man Christ Jesus, who is the most excellent and glorious of all creatures, yet meek and lowly of heart, excels all creatures in humility; for though he is more excellent than any other creature, yet he is more sensible of his own comparative

meanness [lowness] and littleness, when compared with the
divine nature or his infinite distance from that. Humility is one
of the excellencies of Christ because he is not only God, but
man; and so humility is in him as man.[9]

Jesus is our primary example of humility because he knew himself
and God perfectly. In his humanity, he grasped his meekness and
lowness compared to God. Since Jesus the man is personally united
to God, he knew in his humanity the full extent of his finitude and
weakness. But Jesus is not the only example of humility; both the
glorified saints in heaven and the angels shine in superlative humility: "There can be no true humility in any without the creature's
seeing his distance from God, not only with respect to greatness but
also loveliness. The angels and saints in heaven see both."[10] Humility
is an abiding virtue in the lives of all creatures who commune with
their Creator.

Knowing our depravity. When someone fails to acknowledge the
utter depravity of his heart, it's a "red flag" in the Christian life. In
contrast, Paul is the model: "The saying is trustworthy and deserving
of full acceptance, that Christ Jesus came into the world to save
sinners, of whom I am the foremost" (1 Tim 1:15). Edwards shares a
similar sentiment: "It has often appeared to me, that if God should
mark iniquity against me, I should appear the very worst of all
mankind; . . . and that I should have by far the lowest place in hell."[11]
He continues, "When I look into my heart, and take a view of my
wickedness, it looks like an abyss infinitely deeper than hell."[12]

Therefore, the purpose of viewing our depravity is to grasp more
fully onto Christ, who has overcome and conquered sin. It is not to
equate yourself with sin, but is an attempt to take stock of how pervasive sin is in your life. All actions, especially religious or spiritual
actions, are tainted deeply with sin. Spiritual formation entails an
honest and open confession of ourselves before the God who searches

and knows our hearts (Ps 139:1). The only way this knowledge is possible is by a true apprehension of who God is. Everything that is done, achieved, lost or depraved is now viewed in light of God and his glory.[13]

Maturity reimagined. Understanding maturity in this manner is very different than what many assume. For many, the Christian life has been so oriented around themselves and fixing their problems, that "growth" necessarily entails seeing yourself as holy, good and true. Edwards tells us a different story. There are two divergent emphases that drive Edwards's understanding of the Christian life. First is the idea of true growth, which is greater dependence upon God. Second is the idea that as we grow we become more aware of our depravity. In the first instance, it is possible to look back at our early immaturity with awe at how depraved we were. Edwards tells us, "It is affecting to me to think, how ignorant I was, when I was a young Christian, of the bottomless, infinite depths of wickedness, pride, hypocrisy and deceit left in my heart."[14] So there is a sense in which Edwards can look at his life and be amazed at how far he has come in light of where he was when he started. He understands that even though there is a long road ahead, he has also journeyed far. And yet, we have also seen how aware Edwards was of his own heart, and how he had a greater notion of depravity in his maturity than in his immaturity. Note his explanation:

> Though it seems to me, that in some respects I was a far better Christian, for two or three years after my first conversion, than I am now; and lived in a more constant delight and pleasure: yet of late years, I have had a more full and constant sense of the absolute sovereignty of God, and a delight in that sovereignty; and have had more of a sense of the glory of Christ, as a mediator, as revealed in the gospel.[15]

Most spiritual thinkers throughout history have noted this reality, and probably most of us can relate to it. When we are young in the faith we bring a zeal that feels and looks like the epitome of devotion. It is in the midst of this zeal that many young people are thrust into leadership well beyond their maturity and faith. But notice Edwards's description. In his early days of faith he had more "constant delight and pleasure," but in his maturity he realizes much of it was fleshliness dressed up as godliness. In his maturity, he looks, not to his own delight and pleasure, but to his focus and delight in God as all in all. Again, he provides us with a detailed description:

> I have vastly a greater sense, of my universal, exceeding depen-
> dence on God's grace and strength, and mere good pleasure,
> of late, than I used formerly to have; and have experienced
> more of an abhorrence of my own righteousness. The thought
> of any comfort or joy, arising in me, on any consideration, or
> reflection on my own amiableness, or any of my performances
> or experiences, or any goodness of heart or life, is nauseous
> and detestable to me. And yet I am greatly afflicted with a
> proud and self-righteous spirit; much more sensibly, than I
> used to be formerly.[16]

If we use Edwards's life as an example of maturity we see there is a movement of the Spirit to make him dependent on God alone. Alongside that movement was a swing from a pride-filled youth with great pleasure and delight, to a mature adult who was now less full of pride but more aware of his pride than ever before. We see a similar movement in the disciples' lives as well, where Jesus eventually leads them in his teaching to a place where they could finally hear that without him, they could do nothing (Jn 15:5).

This leads us to an important issue in Edwards's legacy. Those readers more familiar with Edwards's life and work will wonder why I have yet to introduce his famous "Resolutions." There is good reason for this. "Resolutions" were a standard practice for educated people in the eighteenth century.[17] Even Benjamin Franklin wrote life resolutions. Edwards famously wrote seventy resolutions for his life, ranging over the broadest possible features of his existence, from eating, resting, studying and praying to time management. Resolutions were often tightly stated commands to oneself about the virtuous life. For instance, Edwards's sixth resolution was, "Resolved, to live with all my might, while I do live."[18] These seventy resolutions were written by the time Edwards was twenty, and are therefore a part of his "zealous" youth. This last point is important in light of what we have noted about Edwards's mature view of his earlier Christian life. While he was young, he was zealous without real abiding spiritual depth. Note the resolution quoted above. There is nothing distinctively "Christian" about this. No doubt Benjamin Franklin had a similar resolution. It is in light of this that we need to take Edwards's comments about his youth seriously: "I used to be continually examining myself, and studying and contriving for likely ways and means, how I should live holily, with far greater diligence and earnestness, than ever I pursued anything in my life: *but with too great a dependence on my own strength; which afterwards proved a great damage to me.*"[19] Edwards looks back through the lens of his maturity and recognizes his use of resolutions as an act of his own independence rather than dependence on God.

This previous statement should give us pause. Possibly the widest read document of Edwards's work is his "Resolutions." The very practice that led him to his own self-willing has become our favorite writing. Three things should become clear to us in light of this. First, as North American evangelicals, we are prone to this very temptation. Probably more than any other temptation, we are often seduced by independence, self-power and our own ability to make things happen. In Edwards's maturity, he saw this for what it was—foolishness—but in his youth, he was zealous without discernment. Second, the "Resolutions" have become so popular, let me suggest, because they are simple. Again, building on the last point, we are constantly tempted to make the Christian life a series of things we can achieve. The resolutions can play into this temptation. Notice the sixth resolution quoted above — it is easier to make action plans through our own self-willing than to rest in the grace and power of God. "Just tell me what to do and I'll do it" is the foundation of much idolatry. Furthermore, the "Resolutions" have led many to rave about the man Jonathan Edwards and how impressive he was. This runs contrary to the Spirit's movement of growth. Edwards would rather have history claim, "Wow, look at the work of the Spirit in that man's life." Third, resolutions are not bad in and of themselves. This is important to emphasize. Resolutions were used in self-examination as tools to turn people to God's strength and not their own. When used in this manner, they can be helpful. Resolutions need to be ordered by grace and oriented to God, and not focused on self-achievement through the zeal of immaturity.

After Edwards's comment about how his practice of the resolutions were self-focused, he goes on to state: "My experience had not then taught me, as it has done since, my extreme feebleness and impotence, every manner of way; and the innumerable and bottomless depths of secret corruption and deceit, that there was in my heart."[20] In his maturity, knowledge of God led to knowledge of self. Knowledge of God led him to see how his spiritual practices were often wielded by his flesh more than by the Spirit. He was able to look back on his life and see how his spiritual formation was often an attempt at fleshly formation — where he was in control and in power of his spiritual growth. Even though his youth seemed to have more zeal, that zeal was saturated with his flesh.

The sovereignty principle. This leads us to what I call the "sovereignty principle." The Reformed, as a group, emphasize the sovereignty of God at every turn. Edwards was no different. Unfortunately, while an emphasis on sovereignty leads to an emphasis on the holiness and justice of God, it also has a tendency to lead, ironically, to pride. In contrast, the sovereignty principle claims that a focus on the sovereignty of God leads to humility. When a focus on sovereignty leads to pride, something has gone wrong; knowledge of God has not led to knowledge of self and instead self-deception reigns.

Often, in Edwards's day and in our own, sovereignty fails to lead to humility because of a focus on getting doctrine "right." Edwards would have said that the focus is on speculative knowledge of God rather than affectionate knowledge. Only the latter is really knowing God, and as such only the latter provides humility. As the situation goes, once people figure out right doctrine, they now stand beside God rather than under his judgment. Instead of constantly standing under the prophetic office of Christ while grasping him as priest, they simply remove themselves from his prophetic glare and aim it at others. Suddenly *they* are sovereign, and they take up the reigns of God's judgment. When this is the case, both sovereignty and humility are sold off for self-exaltation and pride, all of which is done in the name of the sovereign God. We cannot properly wield the sword of the Spirit (Eph 6:17) until we fully feel the weight of that fact that the Spirit wields his sword against us (Heb 4:12-13).[21] The second we fail to recognize that the sword of the Spirit is aimed primarily at us, we undermine the sovereignty principle and pride reigns. No amount of proclaiming "Sovereignty!" at the top of our lungs changes this fact if we continue to undermine that claim with our lives. True grace leads to a greater recognition and awe of how much more grace we need. Rather, more often than not, a sovereign God is proclaimed in the same breath that breathes arrogance, pride and judgment. We undermine sovereignty when we turn doctrine into a checklist and ignore humility as central to orthodoxy.

In light of this, perhaps the best way to judge our humility is when we interact with other Christians who disagree with us. Paul tells us to "do nothing from selfish ambition or conceit, but in humility count others more significant than yourselves" (Phil 2:3).[22] Following our example from above, it is often easier to interact with others from outside God's prophetic glare, and instead judge, attack and undermine them under the name of "truth." This is the sin of choice for the great bulk of young Christians (often fueled by the unaccountability of the Internet). In the absence of wisdom's depth, self-assurance and boasting over others is grasped as a replacement. Zeal and ignorance are unfortunately common bedfellows, and pride and self-love are easily masked through claims of truth, justice and the honor of God. When arrogance, pride and self-love reign, it is clear that sovereignty is not grasped in the heart but is only affirmed in words.

Edwards, deeply troubled by these sins of the heart, understood his role as pastor and brother in Christ to entail helping other Christians navigate the depths of their own sinfulness. For instance, Edwards addresses the sin of envy by analyzing how we tend to hide it under virtuous-looking garments. He lists four ways envy shapes our interactions: We (1) undermine the worthiness of the person we envy; (2) claim that our envy arises from a love to justice; (3) undermine the honor of the person we envy by questioning the use of their prosperity and (4) question if the person we envy is spiritually mature enough for prosperity. Notice that these sins are all clothed with righteousness. Our love of justice gives us the justification for undermining the worthiness of the person we are envious of. We put ourselves in the place of judge—make ourselves sovereign—and under the guise of justice we allow our sin to thrive. We are the ones who wield the sword of the Spirit, completely forgetting that it is aimed primarily at our own hearts first. In response, we might question ourselves by asking when we hear admonitions in sermons, or read these criticisms here, do we first think of others or ourselves?

To know God and to know oneself is to be humble.[23] A right emphasis on sovereignty leads not to arrogance and pride, but to complete dependence. We have seen that Edwards moved from a zealous but self-centered youth to a maturity that grasped God's sovereignty and his own humility. Edwards came to know his own heart. He saw the depths of his wickedness, and that led him to grasp onto God's grace all the more. Importantly, from the example above, Edwards understood his role as pastor as knowing his own heart so he could help others navigate theirs. By knowing his own sin, he was able to walk people through their self-deception. This ability is one of the most forgotten practices in the church today. Here, I turn our attention to self-examination as a foundational practice of spiritual formation.

Self-examination as a foundational practice. We have already seen that knowledge of God demands a healthy knowledge of self. We discuss this here because everything we do in the Christian life depends on our understanding this reality. If we do not, we may fail to see how our virtues are simply vices in disguise. Therefore, one of the most foundational practices of the Christian life is self-examination. Every spiritual practice, to some degree, depends upon this foundation. Even reading the Bible and prayer depend on self-examination; without it these practices morph into tools of the flesh rather than means of grace.

For self-examination to properly function in the lives of disciples, knowledge of God must lead to both honesty and humility. Honesty, in that our call is to be who we actually are before God, because God wants to transform *us* and cannot transform the people we pretend to be (because they do not exist).[24] Humility, because one cannot know God without being humble. True humility is being humble from the heart; it entails a unity of understanding and will. False humility is an attempt, often subconscious, to be humble in understanding alone. Humility in knowledge alone is what Edwards would have called hypocrisy. Unlike how we tend to use the term *hypocrisy*, which is something like pretending to be something you are not, Edwards understood it to entail self-deception. In the case of humility, we tend to deceive ourselves into thinking we are humble by using self-talk to transform ourselves (trying to convince yourself you are humble, most likely after a sermon on humility). Rather, true humility is a proper knowledge of who you are before God (knowledge of God and self), and the will to act according to that knowledge.

Because Edwards knew the depths of his own depravity, he emphasized self-examination as a rhythm of life that helped to undermine hypocrisy. He would even say, "if ever we intend to come to any amendment in our lives, we must begin with consideration [self-examination]; for there is no true religion but what is founded on most deliberate consideration."[25] Consider your life and what drives you.[26] We have already seen some examples of how Edwards did this. He was not satisfied with prayer and praise; he wanted to know what drove that prayer and praise. When he found himself questioning if someone was worthy of something they've received, he traced that into his heart to find envy lurking beneath the surface. As with any means of grace, self-examination is not simply an act done in your own power. Self-examination is done in a posture of receiving from God. Self-examination can easily lead to pride when done out of your own power, even if you unveil serious sin. You do not have to be in the church long to realize that those who can talk honestly about their sin are often upheld as spiritually mature. Rather, the goal is not simply to unveil these things or be honest about them. You are called to unveil yourself to the God who really knows what your heart is like, so that he can unveil *to you* the reality of who you actually are. Edwards admonishes his people against the lie that they are able to open their own eyes.[27] Instead of trying to open your own eyes, come before the God who gives eyes to see and ears to hear (Ps 26:2). Paradoxically, as we see our depravity we come to grasp the depth of salvation more fully and rely on God more completely for his sanctifying presence (for example, Ps 51).

Self-examination isn't, therefore, a practice in itself, but an aspect of many different kinds of practices. The emphasis is to know yourself truly in light of who God is and what God is calling you to. This is why self-examination, without a proper notion of God and salvation, can be very dangerous. The goal is not to lead someone to depression, so that they are so overwhelmed by their sin that they cannot move. Rather, the goal is to turn and abide in Christ. Edwards provides some pastoral advice regarding this: "Draw up no dark conclusions against yourself. Don't give yourself over when God has not given you over."[28] The goal is not to show God that you know you are a sinner and then beat yourself up for it. Many attempt to make penance through examination, showing that they still try to save themselves rather than turning to the cross. Rather, the goal is to be who you are with the God who died for you in the midst of your sin. The goal is to grasp grace as you are rather than as you wish you were.

For many of us, I fear, self-examination seems not to fit so well with the gospel. Doesn't God forget all of our past sins? So why shouldn't we? The worry is that a focus on our past sins undermines our grasp of grace. Edwards thought differently. To continue to fully grasp grace, we need to keep before our hearts and minds the reality of our sin: "So you should be very diligent and particular in searching your past life as well as your present practices that you may be sensible what a life you have lived. . . . Should often be bringing as many particular acts of sin to mind as you can. . . . Endeavouring that none may be hid from you and buried in oblivion."[29] Edwards's worry is that a failure to recall our sins is to grasp independence rather than dependence — self-achievement rather than grace. We can trust that God forgets our sins, but to trust in that fully is to recall them vividly and rejoice in God's gracious forgetfulness (Heb 8:12; 10:17).

Like prayer and Scripture, self-examination is a practice that needs to be integrated in every aspect of life. From the mundane realities of our day-to-day existence to the spiritual excitement we find in spiritual practices, we should seek to have our hearts revealed to God. Sin is a deceiving kind of thing. Sin acts to blind and deaden, such that it skews the compass of our hearts. Self-examination allows us to come to God in the way he calls us—in honesty and humility. Therefore, every situation we find ourselves in becomes an opportunity to have our hearts cracked open to God's pervasive glare. Every circumstance, whether it be one of joy, frustration, fear, mourning or dancing, is an opportunity to pray, "Search me, O God, and know my heart." But oftentimes, that isn't enough. It would be naive to assume we can have a deep knowledge of our own hearts in the hectic pace of our lives. In certain circumstances, Edwards advises that something more radical is necessary:

> Under special difficulties, or when in great need of or great longings after any particular mercies for your self or others, set apart a day of secret fasting and prayer alone; and let the day be spent not only in petitions for the mercies you desired, but in searching your heart, and looking over your past life, and confessing your sins before God not as is wont to be done in public prayer, but by a very particular rehearsal before God, of the sins of your past life from your childhood hitherto, before and after conversion, with particular circumstances and aggravations, also very particularly and fully as possible, spreading all the abominations of your heart before him.[30]

Ultimately, the goal of self-examination is to be fully open before God. Self-examination is an act with the Spirit to uncover sin, so that you can hold it before God and seek his grace. Going back to my example of the sword of the Spirit turned on us, it is helpful to note Hebrews 4:12-13: "For the word of God is living and active, sharper than any two-edged sword, piercing to the division of soul and of spirit, of joints and of marrow, and discerning the thoughts and intentions of the heart. And no creature is hidden from his sight, but all are naked and exposed to the eyes of him to whom we must give account." Self-examination is not an exercise of self-will, but a means of grace where we open to the work of the Spirit to search us and know us, to penetrate to the depths of our beings and hold open our hearts to the grace of God. In self-examination we penetrate to the depths of our hearts as an act of presenting ourselves as living sacrifices. We seek not to be conformed to the world, but transformed by the renewing of our minds (Rom 12:1-2). Only by the grace of God will we not think more highly of ourselves than we ought to think, but will think with sober judgment (Rom 12:3), not being deceived by the sin that muddies our perception.

Rather than leading to fear, self-examination is done in freedom because God has given us his grace. God already knows the sins we are so hesitant to unveil. When we reveal our hearts before God we are revealing to God only small portions of the depravity he sees within us—and yet he died for us within that depravity, while we were still sinners (Rom 5:8). The practice of self-examination is a humble admission that: "The heart is deceitful above all things, and desperately sick; who can understand it?" (Jer 17:9). It is also an admission that God is ultimately the one who searches the heart, and therefore our call is to be open to the reality that God sees (Jer 17:10). It is along these lines that Edwards eventually came to admit:

> I once did not imagine that the heart of man had been so unsearchable as I find it is. I am less charitable, and less uncharitable than once I was. I find more things in wicked men that may counterfeit, and make a fair show of piety, and more ways that the remaining corruption of the godly may make them appear like carnal men, formalists and dead hypocrites, than once I knew of. The longer I live, the less I wonder that God challenges it as his prerogative to try the hearts of the children of men, and has directed that this business should be let alone till the harvest. I find that God is wiser than men.[31]

CONCLUSION

There can be no humility without a true knowledge of yourself, and humility is one of the most foundational virtues in Christianity. To have and maintain the posture of receiving from God, which is the posture of the means of grace, we must know God and know the depth of our own hearts. But true humility is not available by just any kind of knowledge; it must be affectionate knowledge. Humility flows forth from the person who knows *and* loves God, because the love of God unveils the reality of our own sinfulness and rejection of him.[32] Humility is only had by love, through an affectionate knowledge of the God who gave his Son in love.

The world in which we live is designed to thwart a deep knowledge of ourselves. Advertisers play on our temptations, death seems impossible, and we are constantly presented with infinite options at our disposal. Edwards's world was different. Death was constant. Death did not occur in hospitals, but on couches in homes. War was always on their doorstep, and attack always seemed imminent. The world had no real sustainability. The world slipped through their fingers so fast it was difficult to grasp. Their world was passing away, and as it did they caught glimpses of the eternal lurking beneath the surface. Knowing the depths of our own hearts—our temptations, blindness, fear, anger and fleshliness—allows us to be present to the reality that our life is hidden with Christ in God (Col 3:3). It turns us away from ourselves and onto grace. Self-examination is a way to come to the cross and cry out for grace and mercy, trusting that the Holy Spirit too is crying out from within us with "groanings too deep for words" (Rom 8:26).

6

Meditation and Contemplation

True religion disposes persons to be much alone,
in solitary places, for holy meditation and prayer.

JONATHAN EDWARDS, *RELIGIOUS AFFECTIONS*

One thing I have asked of the LORD, that will I seek after: that I may
dwell in the house of the LORD all the days of my life, to gaze upon
the beauty of the LORD and to inquire in his temple.

PSALM 27:4

IF YOU COULD ASK A PASTOR IN Edwards's day if a Christian should be involved in meditation and contemplation, "Of course!" would be the obvious response. The idea that a Christian would not practice meditation or contemplation would have been nothing short of baffling. Today is different. Unfortunately, for many, the terms *meditation* and *contemplation* have become tied up with New Age or Eastern mysticism. The words themselves seem tainted by unchristian ideologies. We have already seen this same tendency with words like *spirituality* and *spiritual formation*. Instead of being faithful to practice these in a distinctively Christian and evangelical manner, we capitulate to outside forces and flail about for new terms to use. In turn, division arises in the church as some look down on others who employ this terminology, all while others invoke them in an elitist manner. This endless circle of foolishness has caught many in its trap (2 Tim 2:14). This is exactly the kind of thing Edwards expected to happen when people devote themselves more deeply to God—Satan comes in and tries to deceive, confuse and muddle the Christian life by creating false teachings that mimic Christian ones.

The appropriate response to these scenarios is to dig deeply into Christian teaching on the need and use of proper meditation and contemplation. This chapter does just that, looking at Edwards's life and ideals as an example. I situate this chapter here because meditation and contemplation are foundational postures for the means of grace I address in the next chapter. Meditation and contemplation act as the mortar in the foundation of Scripture and prayer. Thomas Manton, a theologian Edwards read, claimed, "Meditation is a middle sort of duty between the word and prayer, and hath respect to both. The word feedeth meditation, and meditation feedeth prayer; . . . These duties must always go hand in hand; meditation must follow hearing and precede prayer."[1] We must do more than read the Word; we must digest it, and that digestion fuels prayer. Along with self-examination, meditation and contemplation are foundational because they should saturate the Christian life as a whole. These practices are forms of prayer and hearing Scripture that govern our Christian existence built on Christ.

THE NATURE OF MEDITATION

While the broader scope of meditation is a bit more difficult to understand, at its core, it is exactly what we think it is—intently focusing our mind on a spiritual issue. While this definition is correct, it is not very helpful (practically speaking). In the generations leading up to Edwards it was assumed that meditation was "a steadfast bending of the mind to some spiritual matter, discoursing of it with our selves, till we bring the same to some profitable issue."[2] Inherent to meditation is wrestling with the truth your mind is attending to. It is coming to grips with our sinful and rebellious heart as it recollects God's truth. The goal is not just to think hard about something, but to have that idea raise your affections. Meditation, therefore, is not a single act, but entails several different means of grace. For instance, after considering the death of Christ you would turn to soliloquy. Soliloquy is a method of prayer whereby you speak to both God and your own soul as you hold it before him (there will be more on this in the next chapter). This prayer is modeled after the psalmists who preach to their own souls in the presence of God. Think back to Psalm 42. In the middle of a prayer the psalmist proclaims, "Why are you cast down, O my soul, and why are you in turmoil within me? Hope in God; for I shall again praise him, my salvation and my God" (Ps 42:5-6). In meditation you turn to your stubborn soul and point it to the truth. Likewise, throughout your time of meditation, and specifically as you conclude, you turn to prayer and praise.[3]

Meditation is necessary because Christianity demands more than just abstract knowledge; it entails affectionate knowledge. Edwards wove these ideas together around the idea of beauty, so that our spiritual life progressed through a clearer and clearer vision of divine things. The Spirit illumines the real world to us, so that the false world of the flesh, sin and death fade away. Meditation is attending deeply to God's truth, purposes and revelation, so that the lies of the world are seen as lies, and so the truth of God can pervade every aspect of our lives. The goal is beyond our power, as in all means of grace, but our role is offering to God our meditation that he might

endow us with grace to grasp his way as beautiful.[4] By illuminating
our minds and hearts we grasp the truth of God's beauty and glory.
Meditation saturates us in God's truth because it goes beyond mere
glimpses of truth. Rather than reading Scripture quickly only to
move on and think about other things, meditation involves a careful
and deep attending, often compared to chewing and digesting.

Puritans and Meditation: Edwards's Spiritual Culture

Having in our minds the broad picture of meditation, we now turn
to more specific issues. For the Puritans, meditation is broken down
into two main situations: occasional and deliberate.[5] In occasional
meditation, the fodder for your meditation is whatever you are doing,
experiencing and seeing. This is a recognition that God is always
present and unveiling and that his Spirit illuminates his truth. This
meditation depends upon a deep knowledge of Scripture because
Scripture is the grammar of God's revelation. Scripture teaches us
God's language of grace, and meditation uses that to see ourselves,
others and the world. Saturating ourselves with Scripture allows us
to see all beauty as pointing beyond itself to the beauty of God.

The second kind of meditation is deliberate meditation. Here,
there is a certain time set apart for meditation with a specific Bible
passage, truth or reality to meditate upon. Deliberate meditation
fuels occasional meditation. This focused, silent and devoted act
lays the groundwork for a life of prayer, contemplation and obedience. As Paul wrote to the Corinthians, "For this light momentary
affliction is preparing for us an eternal weight of glory beyond all
comparison, as we look not to the things that are seen but to the
things that are unseen. For the things that are seen are transient, but
the things that are unseen are eternal" (2 Cor 4:17-18). Meditation
mirrors the reality of this "slight momentary affliction." Instead of
waiting for trials, we take it on ourselves to fight against the world
and our flesh so our hearts might focus on the things that are eternal.

Likewise, as Paul writes, "The natural person does not accept the things of the Spirit of God, for they are folly to him, and he is not able to understand them because they are spiritually discerned" (1 Cor 2:14). Even believers have a fleshliness still ingrained in their hearts, blinding their spiritual vision with flesh. Meditation is an assault on that fleshliness. Edwards, along these lines, tells us that he

> set apart days of meditation on particular subjects; as sometimes, to set apart a day for the consideration of the greatness of my sins; at another, to consider the dreadfulness and certainty, of the future misery of ungodly men; at another, the truth and certainty of religion; and so, of the great future things promised and threatened in the Scriptures.[6]

Notice the focus on eternity in Edwards's encouragement for meditation. Setting your mind as far forward as possible provides for greater perspective (Mt 5:12). This is an exercise in calibrating our internal compass. The enemy of meditation is, therefore, a wandering and occupied mind. For our culture, this kind of mind is pervasive. It is not calm, collected and ordered, but is chaotic, restless and unceasing. Meditation and contemplation will necessitate, and encourage, a focused heart. That said, when your mind does wander, meditation grabs those thoughts and brings them before God. It is in the midst of lustful thoughts, anxiousness and boredom that the fruitfulness of meditation is known. Meditation assumes a sinful heart. The response is not to work hard at overcoming a wandering mind (self-help) but to bring those thoughts before the God who has provided peace in his Son. A calm heart is not a sinless heart, but one that knows forgiveness in Christ Jesus. It rests in God's work and not its own. Notice that meditation and contemplation fit within a very specific picture of the Christian life. God's work in sanctification calms the soul, a calm that can be contrasted with the chaos of the world. Unfortunately, this calmness comes at a price. Our hearts are in rebellion. Our hearts desire chaos. In capitulating, even if we attempt to baptize this chaos for Christian purposes, what we are doing is handing our souls to the world:

> For the vanities of the world, you have neglected reading, praying, and meditation: for the things of the world, you have broken the sabbath: for the world you have spent a great deal of your time in quarrelling: for the world you have envied, and hated your neighbor: for the world you have cast God, and Christ, and heaven behind your back: for the world you have sold your own soul: you have as it were drowned your soul in worldly cares and desires: you have been a mere earthworm, that is never in its element but when grovelling and buried in the earth.[7]

As with the foundational postures we have already discussed, meditation is a practice that encompasses all of life. It is a call to be thoughtful and attentive to the God who loves you. Meditation of this nature is based on the belief that Christ is all in all—that our lives need to be saturated with the reality of God and his call. As one scholar puts it, "Meditation was a daily duty that enhanced every other duty of the Puritan's Christian life. As oil lubricates an engine, so meditation facilitates the diligent use of means of grace . . . , deepens the marks of grace (repentance, faith, humility), and strengthens one's relationship to others (love to God, to fellow Christians, to one's neighbors at large)."[8] Meditation is the initial response to love God "with all your heart and with all your soul and with all your mind and with all your strength" (Mk 12:30).

BIBLICAL BACKDROP FOR MEDITATION

The Puritan meditation tradition looked to Isaac as the model for meditation. We are told in Genesis that "Isaac went out to meditate in the field toward evening" (Gen 24:63), and his example was often suggested to others, both to meditate and to do so "toward evening."⁹ But this, of course, is not the only passage to encourage meditation. After Moses' death, the Lord calls Joshua into his service. The Lord tells him, "This Book of Law shall not depart from your mouth, but you shall meditate on it day and night, so that you may be careful to do according to all that is written in it" (Josh 1:8). Likewise, Psalms tells us that the blessed person is the one whose "delight is in the law of the LORD, and on his law he meditates day and night" (Ps 1:2). Furthermore, David exclaims, "My soul will be satisfied as with fat and rich food, and my mouth will praise you with joyful lips, when I remember you upon my bed, and meditate on you in the watches of the night" (Ps 63:5-6). More specifically, he narrates in another psalm, "I remember the days of old; I meditate on all that you have done; I ponder the work of your hands" (Ps 143:5). These passages reveal that meditation is not simply on the Bible, but includes God and his works. Likewise, once we are given "eyes to see" in conversion, the Lord teaches us the language of grace and faith so that we can "read" who he is in everything. As I already quoted, Edwards claims, "I am not ashamed to own that I believe that the whole universe, heaven and earth, air and seas, and the divine constitution and history of the holy Scriptures, be full of images of divine things, as full as a language is of words."¹⁰ The holy Scriptures ground meditation so we may know the language of the gospel and "read" God's presence everywhere. The foundation of meditation, therefore, is a careful, diligent attending to the divine Word. Edwards admonishes his people:

> The chapter [Romans 12] is well worth our most diligent and frequent reading, and that we should bind the words and rules thereof, that we should bind them upon our hearts; yea, that they should be written in indelible characters there, that it should be the object of continual meditation, lying down and

rising up, and that we should frequently examine our lives by it, as by an excellent catalog of those duties and practices, which, if performed, will make us appear Christians indeed, and will mold our hearts and regulate our lives according to Jesus Christ and his image.[11]

Notice that the reading of Scripture, which we can assume as deliberative meditation (a time set apart for this practice), fuels occasional meditation. The Word orients your vision so you should be in "continual meditation"; it forms your vision of reality, and it molds your heart according to the image of Christ.

Just as attending to the written Word spurs deeper and more continual reflection, so our role in Sunday services is to instigate this same reaction. It is in Sunday services "especially that his saints do feed upon him in meditation, hearing his Word, and partaking of the sacrament of the Lord's Supper."[12] In taking the Lord's Supper we are "feeding upon him in meditation." The sermon is the preached word and the supper is the visual word that orient the eyes of our hearts to *the* Word—Christ (Jn 1:14). As we faithfully set our minds on the sermon and the supper we are setting before our hearts the truth, grace and beauty of God for the "eye of our soul" to behold. "We should take care, therefore, to employ our minds on a sabbath day on spiritual objects, by holy meditation, improving for our help therein the holy Scriptures and other books that are according [to] the Word of God."[13]

EDWARDS ON MEDITATION

Edwards told his church to set their minds on things of a divine nature and to turn the eye of their minds toward them, "that these highest glories that can be thought [of], might be more the objects of their meditation!"[14] The "eye of your mind" links the idea of meditation to the visual. As the Christian life is a journey to see clearly, meditation is attending deeply to the beauty and glory of God. This is not "physical" sight—we do not see new objects. Rather, the "eye of our minds" is able to see reality for what it truly is. As Spirit-indwelt believers we now grasp the beauty of reality and the ugliness of depravity. Our posture in meditation is to receive grace to be formed according to this beauty—the beauty of God—that the ways of God become our ways. It is here that we seek the path of the Lord by seeking the Lord himself (Ps 5:8). Meditation is, therefore, an activity of the heart (Ps 4:4; Lk 2:19). As an activity that seeks to unite the understanding and the will to an affectionate knowledge of God (an activity of the heart), meditation is necessarily rational:

> When we meditate, then we act as reasonable creatures, then reason acts, then the soul is in exercise. Shall we have souls within us, and let them lie dead without any exercise? We ought to spend much time in meditation; we ought to meditate on God's Word day and night (Psalm 1:2). The law of God should be a constant companion to converse with, lying down and rising up, and wherever we are.[15]

This is not how we tend to see rationality. This is not racking our brains around an idea trying to figure it out. Instead, in meditation we are "exercising" our minds according to their true created purpose—to gaze upon the glory and beauty of God. As pilgrims, this knowledge does not come easily. We focus our minds to try and understand Scripture, but we do so as a means of grace. This is not in our power but in a posture of dependence upon God. Edwards tells us, "Our understandings were given us to be used, and above all to be exercised, in divine things. Therefore God teaches us in such a way that we shall have some exercise of meditation and study. God gives us the gold, but he gives it to us in a mine that we might dig for it."[16] In meditation, we pour over how God has presented himself in Scripture, in redemption history, in the world and in our lives, and

we hold that before God in light of who we are. This is why meditation ties together the Word, prayer and knowledge of God and ourselves. Meditation is where we hold these together before the prophetic gaze of Christ. Meditation leads us from Scripture to prayer
because meditation is more than reading for information, but is
learning from God in the reality of our own lives. For Edwards, meditation was a constant necessity of living in God's world. Edwards
talks about how he used to "praise God, by singing psalms in prose,
and by singing forth the meditations of my heart in prose."[17]
Throughout, and in closing, a time of meditation one would pray
and praise God. There was not a specific model (do X, Y and Z in
this specific order), but the whole purpose of meditation was to set
one's mind and heart on Christ and his truth.

Meditating on Christ. In one of Edwards's sermons, he outlines
a meditation on Christ. Doing so provides a framework to use for
meditating on Christ on one's own. This was typical for Puritan
sermons.[18] The sermon was an example for people concerning how
they should handle their own souls. The pastor's shepherding was
the prime example for private soul care. Edwards provides eight emphases in his meditation: First, "Consider how proper it is that Christ
should have dominion and power, who is the great God's only Son
and heir."[19] Edwards knows the human heart. He realizes how quick
and easy it is for one's heart to grow forgetful of who Christ truly is.
Starting with Christ's proper dominion and power, Edwards grounds
our meditation on Christ in Christ's true nature as God's own Son.

Second, "Consider what it was that moved him ever to become
the king of the children of men." Edwards goes on to tell us that love
moved Christ to become our deliverer. "His heart [y]earned towards
us; it was a time of love with him. Being of an infinitely gracious
nature, [he] was pleased to love us with a very dear love; his delights
were with the sons of men (Prov. 8:31)."[20] Building on who God is in
himself, Edwards turns to who God is *for us.* We do not know an

absent-mindedly transcendent God, but one who has come to us in love as Christ Jesus.

Third, "Consider that Christ lays the foundation of this kingdom of his in his blood."[21] Turning more specifically to who God is *for us* in his work on the cross, Edwards focuses on Christ's suffering. The Christ we are to love is the Christ who first loved us and laid down his life for us (1 Jn 4:19).

Fourth, "Consider the excellency of the laws and rules by which Christ's kingdom is governed."[22] Edwards turns from Christ himself to the nature of his reign. Just as Christ is beautiful and excellent, so is his reign over creatures. His "yoke is easy, and [his] burden is light" (Mt 11:30).

Fifth, "Consider the excellent and gracious manner of Christ's governing his people by communicating vital influences to them and governing their hearts." These "vital influences" that govern the heart are Christ's working graciously through the Spirit in the hearts of his people. "Christ don't drive, but he draws the heart; he draws by light and love," Edwards proclaims.[23] God does not override his people, forcing them to submission. Rather, in Christ, God draws his people to himself by revealing the excellence, beauty and majesty of Christ. As Edwards moves through each level of the meditation he is attempting to open our hearts in awe of the God who has faithfully sought us in Christ. He wields the logic of the gospel so that our hearts will bow in praise and adoration.

Sixth, "Compare this dominion of Christ that believers are under to the tyranny of that master that the rest of the world are under."[24] Here Edwards turns his attention from his proper subject—Christ— to further reveal Christ's excellence by highlighting its opposite. Satan's reign of deception opposes Christ's, not only in content, value and goal, but also in how their dominions are run. Christ seeks to open eyes to see his beauty; Satan seeks to blind people with worldliness. By noting Satan, Christ's beauty appears brighter.

Seventh, "Consider the end of Christ's rule and dominion over his people in another world."[25] Taking his last point one step further, Edwards focuses on the perfection of Christ's reign in heaven (Neh 9:6). We have already seen what this entails in the first section. Edwards wants his people to set their minds on heaven so that all else will appear dim in the light of God's glorious communion with his saints. We are citizens of that world of love (Phil 3:20); therefore our hearts should feel at home there now.

Last, "The angels count it their happiness that Christ is king over them. How they sing."[26] I have already noted that the Puritans liked to end their meditation with praise; Edwards does so by focusing on the angels. Why? The angels offer us a distinct point of view—beings who know no sin and who gaze upon God eternally. The angels provide a glimpse of what God's presence is like. Furthermore, if your heart still isn't fully drawn to the reign of God, this is another prod. Edwards is subtly saying, "Look, the angels know perfection and yet glorify God and praise his name. They bask in the rule of God and do not buck against it." Edwards ends with a verse to guide their praise: "And I beheld, and I heard the voice of many angels round about the throne and the beasts and the elders: and the number of them was ten thousand times ten thousand, and thousands of thousands; saying with a loud voice, 'Worthy is the Lamb that was slain to receive power, and riches, and wisdom, and strength, and honour, and glory, and blessing'" (Rev 5:11-12).[27]

Notice the flow of Edwards's meditation. He starts with God's nature, moves to the incarnation and crucifixion, and turns to the nature and governance of God's rule in Christ. He then compares Christ's rule and governance to Satan's, only to turn his attention back to the perfection of Christ's reign in heaven and the angelic witness to that reign. He starts with God's inner life and moves to God's life with his people for eternity. His focus is on God redeeming a people for himself. This is the vision that captures his attention. It is this story that he holds before his heart, so his heart will grasp the beauty and perfection of God. Elsewhere, in encouraging his people to keep to the "exercises of religion," he states, "We are especially to meditate upon and celebrate the work of redemption. We are especially joyfully to remember the resurrection of Christ, because that was Christ finishing the work of redemption."[28] We focus on the resurrection because it carries within it the whole work of Christ. It is *this Christ* who has ascended and sits at the right hand of the Father, *this Christ* now available in faith and therefore *this Christ* on whom we must set our minds. Edwards tells us that a believer, "by fixing his meditations on Christ," is able to commune with him. If we want to have affectionate communion with Christ, it is "necessary that we should fix our meditations on him." Christ "calls us to that end." Furthermore, "Christ should be the chief object of a believer's contemplations as he is the most worthy and glorious object."[29] By offering this meditation on Christ in a sermon, Edwards provided an oral example of what private meditation should look like. Importantly, the focal point of the meditation was on Christ—both his person and work—and was holding before one's heart his beauty, truth and goodness.

Conclusion. Before turning our attention to contemplation, let me conclude by quickly pointing to some aspects of meditation not yet covered. First, Edwards tended to make his argument for meditation based upon the commonsensical reality that when we love something, we set our minds upon it: "When men would discover anything in human arts, they set themselves to study upon it."[30] How much more so with the God of glory and beauty? Second, and building on our first point, we need to watch the excuses of our hearts in our neglect of meditation. Edwards admonishes himself, "I seem to be afraid, after errors and decays, to give myself the full exercise of spiritual meditation: not to give way to such fears."[31] Edwards recognizes a vicious circle that occurs with sin or laziness—we refuse to get back into spiritual activity because we are afraid or too guilt-ridden to face God. Edwards encourages us to seek after the God of grace. Last, once again building on the previous, meditation pulls together all of the spiritual themes discussed in this book thus far. Meditation entails knowing both God and ourselves, and having eyes to see and gaze upon God's beauty. Notice Edwards's further encouragements to himself:

> As a help against that inward shameful hypocrisy, to confess frankly to myself all that which I find in myself, either infirmity or sin; also to confess to God, and open the whole case to him . . . , and humbly and earnestly implore of him the help that is needed; not in the least to endeavor to smother over what is in my heart, but to bring it all out to God and my conscience. By this means, I may arrive at a greater knowledge of my own heart.[32]

Notice that Edwards ties a deep knowledge of his own heart to the task of meditation. Meditation is a wrestling with God and his truth, such that knowing your own temptations, sins, blind spots and frailty are essential to speaking the truth into the core of your being.

CONTEMPLATION OF DIVINE THINGS

Contemplation, no less than meditation, is imperative for the Christian life. There are two main examples. First is the heavenly example, and second is the example of Christ. Those who have gone to be with the Lord are contemplating his glory, beauty and perfection. Therefore, as we prepare for eternity, we ponder those things now. Edwards tells us that the "great part of that work of a Christian ought to be contemplation. That will be the work of every Christian in another world [i.e., heaven] and every Christian should get so much knowledge that he may be able to give everyone, render to everyone, a reason of his religion" (1 Pet 3:15).[33] The key here is that "religion" is a true relationship with God, a relationship that demands the sight of God offered in faith. The saints in heaven know "religion in its highest perfection," Edwards tells us. They are "exceedingly affected with what they behold and contemplate, of God's perfections and works. They are all as a pure heavenly flame of fire, in their love."[34] The glorified saints in heaven contemplate God. But why? Three reasons: "1. Without this they could not glorify God. 2. By this they shall enjoy God. 3. By this means they shall make progress in glorifying and enjoying God."[35]

The reality of our glorified brothers and sisters contemplating God helps ground why we do it here. First, without contemplation God cannot be glorified. Why? God redeems and reconciles his people to himself as we truly are—as people. "Man is distinguished from the inferior creatures," Edwards explains, "in that he is a creature endowed with such faculties as capacitate him for contemplation. Faculties will be brought to the highest perfection."[36] Humans were created with the specific capacities to see God and therefore know him personally. The goal of human persons is to know and love God. The perfection of humanity, therefore, is found when those capacities are in perfect exercise. Likewise, even though we will not know the perfection of our human capacity before glory, we are called to exercise those faculties according to the plan and will of God. This is contemplation. Second, we are told that it is by contemplation that we will enjoy God. Again, why? In our contemplation in heaven we are "pure fire" because we are perfectly attuned to our created purpose. Heaven is where people come to know what they were created for. Existing according to your created design is being made happy—truly happy. In contemplation we come to understand that God has created us to know and to love. This existence is the height of satisfaction and delight. Third, we are told that we will make progress in glorifying and enjoying God for eternity. Our eternal life is a life of ever-increasing delight and enjoyment of God. Even though we will always have complete satisfaction, our

capacity will always grow. This increasing knowledge and love of
God is only possible through a pure and unhindered gazing upon
God's beauty, glory and perfection. It is this sight that serves as an
example for our life now. We see through a glass darkly, but we see
nonetheless. Therefore, in faith, we gaze upon God.

In this life, therefore, we practice contemplation as we anticipate
our eternal life with God. To our second point: Jesus, in his earthly
life, is our example:

> His great devotion, his neglect of the applause of the multitude,
> his forsaking it to converse with God alone, etc. (see also Luke
> 4:42). He delighted to retreat from these things to spend time
> alone in divine contemplation, prayer and converse with God,
> so as to spend great part of the night, so depriving himself of
> sleep all that night, spending it in acts of devotion & mercy
> (Luke 6:12).[37]

Jesus, even in his sinless perfection, created space for silence, solitude and contemplation of God. While we struggle with our identity
in Christ, often failing to grasp our identity as sons and daughters,
Jesus perfectly understood his identity as *the* Son. Even with this
perfect understanding he created space to contemplate the divine
reality. In fact, grasping his identity surely led him to contemplation.
Just like the saints in heaven, Jesus knew who he was and therefore
fixated his sight on God the Father. Jesus' example is ours to grasp
and use as a prod to contemplating God. Edwards encourages us:
"God is the saints to be enjoyed by them. His divine glory and beauty
is for them to behold and be happy in the contemplation of [him]."[38]
As we receive this call to contemplation, the obvious question that
needs to be addressed is, What is contemplation?

What is contemplation? Meditation and contemplation are
really two sides of the same coin. They both entail focusing one's
mind and heart on a specific idea. Simply put, contemplation

is "the action of beholding, or looking at with attention and thought."[39] But, of course, this is a very simple definition for a much deeper reality. Contemplation of God is for the purpose of being alive to him. Therefore, here I outline what it is to "contemplate divine things."

Building on our previous discussion concerning means of grace, it is helpful to recall that grace works itself out in two different ways. There are immanent acts of grace and practical acts of grace. In immanent acts of grace, such as contemplation, the outcome is the heart. Rather than creating a new practical reality (maybe helping someone in need), this act of grace recalibrates the heart. By helping to form the heart, immanent acts of grace *do* lead to practices. They do so indirectly. Practical acts of grace, on the other hand, lead directly to a specific action.[40] Contemplation, therefore, is setting your mind on God for the formation of your heart. "The mind is instructed and led on in its contemplations [by grace] to enlightening views of things (Ps. 16:7; Ps. 63:5-6)." Christ speaks into the soul and excites "holy affections, suggesting ideas, and divine views to our minds." This divine conversation in the soul "engages the mind in contemplation on such things that are of the most entertaining, delightful, and satisfying [nature]."[41] Again we see grace engaging the soul in conversation, but now, pointing to God and his beauty. This grace is simply Christ, by his Spirit, unveiling and revealing himself there. By grace, our mind can focus on the things of God.

This is why the "business of a Christian ought to be very much [in] contemplation and the improvement of the faculties of his mind in divine things."[42] The mind and soul were created to have God as their main object of affection. When this happens, the soul is "at rest," not because it is inactive, but because it is functioning in its sweet spot. This rest is not inactivity, but is perfect activity. This is why we are told:

In Christ you shall have glorious objects for the eye of your soul to behold in which you shall find rest. You shall have glorious objects of your understanding and contemplation. The glories of God and beauty of Christ shall be the objects of your view and the way of salvation by Christ will be like a green pasture for your soul to feed on. And the glorious gospel with its various excellent doctrines and divine truths shall be as a garden to your soul set with a variety of pleasant plants, flowers, and fruits that are ravishing to the eye. In the pleasure that you will have in beholding those lovely objects, your soul shall have sweet rest. . . . The beauty and glory that is seen is sweet enough you will never desire to see anything more beautiful.[43]

Contemplation is actively setting your mind on the beauty and glory of God. The main difference between meditation and contemplation is that in meditation both divine truth *and* your own soul are the objects. In meditation, you are constantly going back and forth between the truth of divine reality and the truth of your own sinfulness. Meditation is taking a specific truth of God and standing before it so the truth of your life comes to view. There is a twofold goal in meditation—to know God and to know oneself. You are wrapped up in yourself in meditation in a way that is not true in contemplation. Notice how contemplation is described:

A true saint, when in the enjoyment of true discoveries of the sweet glory of God and Christ, has his mind too much captivated and engaged by what he views without himself, to stand at that time to view himself, and his own attainments: it would be a diversion and loss which he could not bear, to take his eye off from the ravishing object of his contemplation, to survey his own experience, and to spend time in thinking with himself, what an high attainment this is, and what a good story I now have to tell others.[44]

Furthermore, "Grace in lively exercise shuts out vain thoughts and engages and fixes it in contemplation on those things that are of the most noble nature and highest concerns concerning the supreme being." In contemplation your mind is so captivated by the object of beauty—God in Christ—that all of your effort is expended in receiving that beauty. We do not experience this as hard work but as rest. Think about gazing on a sunset or a magnificent snow-covered mountain range. Focusing on this is a kind of work. Your mind is captivated and you will yourself to keep looking, but you do not see it as work. The sight gives rest to your soul. This, in a small way, is like gazing upon the beauty and glory of God in Christ.

Therefore, unlike meditation, contemplation is not an attempt to focus on a specific sin or area of your life that is not conformed to God. In meditation, the primary aim is attending to divine truth, but you always do so in light of who you are as the person who doesn't fully grasp that truth. In contemplation, you only seek God; you set your mind on Christ for his sake alone. Contemplation is the primary action of the person who proclaims, "To God be the glory." A failure to grasp this call is a failure to believe in God's glory alone. In this sense, contemplation is the capstone of all means of grace. It is still a kind of prayer, as all means of grace are, because you are coming to God and sitting at his feet with full attention. Contemplation is being Mary, at the feet of Jesus, not allowing the worries and anxieties of the world to diminish her devotion (Lk 10:38-42).

The nature of setting one's mind on Christ. I have thus far used a lot of visual imagery to talk about contemplation, so much so that you may have the wrong idea. Contemplation is not receiving a vision from God. The vision of God is only had in heaven. In contemplation you are given a new sense of the glory and beauty of truths you may already know (or are just learning). In this sense, contemplation builds on meditation and the other means of grace, and it will feed back into your practice to spur you on to greater devotion:

Many persons are slack and negligent. . . . They don't daily
exercise themselves as they ought to do in contemplation on
Christ and the glorious things of the Gospel. They don't apply
themselves as they ought by meditation and prayer and diligent
searching the word of God and other books that tend to explain it to see more and more of the glories and wonders of
Jesus Christ. The business of a Christian ought to be very
much [in] contemplation and the improvement of the faculties of his mind in divine things.[45]

Notice the emphasis. Many fail to focus their minds at all, and
therefore neglect the gift God has for them—a realization of his
glory and beauty. Many are so focused on practical means of grace,
on doing things for God, that they fail to realize God wants to form
their hearts through a vision of his beauty. We sell our soul to prag-
matics, and before we realize it we are simply trying hard to generate
holiness. Instead, we need to "seek the things that are above, where
Christ is, seated at the right hand of God" (Col 3:1). We need to have
a sight of God's truth, glory and beauty to pry our eyes off the world
and help us see the world for what it is. Without this sight, without a
devotion to contemplation, we will inevitably baptize worldliness
without realizing it.

In Edwards's own experience, we see that a focus on contemplation leads to deeper meditation: "I had an inward, sweet sense of
these things, that at times came into my heart; and my soul was led
away in pleasant views and contemplations of them. And my mind
was greatly engaged, to spend my time in reading and meditating on
Christ; and the beauty and excellency of his person."[46] First, contemplation leads to more meditation (and vice versa), more wrestling
with God and his truth. Second, because of this meditation, God is
gracious enough to give us times where we are "led away" to a more
pure gazing upon him. This gazing is always through a glass darkly,

but it is clear enough to captivate our hearts. As we saw in the first section, this gazing is the pilgrim-anticipation of the beatific-glory we behold in heaven. Because our vision now is through a glass darkly, we do not have these ideas clearly set forth in our minds. The "level" of contemplation, therefore, ebbs and flows. Edwards tells us that "the ideas we have of things by contemplation, are much stronger and clearer, than at other times."[47] This should be expected. In glorification our sight will be clear and ravishing because it will be immediately before us—we will see God "face to face" (1 Cor 13:12). Here, however, we see God through his actions in the world and his truth. We see God through our remembrance of Christ and his work in the world.

One of the main differences, Edwards tells us, between the minds of animals and humans is that humans can willfully contemplate ideas in their mind.[48] We can call forth memories and attend to them. We call this our imagination. This should not be understood as "imaginary," in the sense of making up a reality that is not true. Rather, the imagination is our ability to call forth images and ideas in our minds. Therefore, there is no meditation or contemplation without imagination:

> I dare appeal to any man, of the greatest powers of mind, whether or no he is able to fix his thoughts on God or Christ, or the things of another world, without imaginary ideas attending his meditations? And the more engaged the mind is, and the more intense the contemplation and affection, still the more lively and strong will the imaginary idea ordinarily be; especially when the contemplation and affection of the mind is attended with anything of surprise; as when the view a person has is very new, and takes strong hold of the passions, either fear or joy; and when the change of the state and views of the mind is sudden, from a contrary extreme, as from that which

was extremely dreadful, to that which is extremely ravishing and delightful.[49]

You need to focus on the reality of Christ and his beauty for contemplation to be contemplation. Therefore, at the heart of both contemplation and spirituality is the reality that one's mind needs rest and focus. In fact, we can say that rest and focus are the same thing. Setting one's mind on Christ entails, necessarily, not focusing on worldliness. If we could somehow bring Edwards through time to our present day, this would no doubt be at the heart of his critique of our culture. Our minds are "tossed to and fro by the waves" (Eph 4:14) of the world and therefore not equipped to receive a sight of the beauty and glory of God. We often equate busyness with achievement, rather than seeing a divided mind as a result of our divided heart. We often confuse the way from above versus the way from below (Jas 3:15-18). Edwards's call to contemplation is a call to focus our minds and hearts on God above all else. This focusing is at the heart of the recalibration noted throughout this book. Contemplation, above all else, is the nature of recalibrating one's whole being around the true north that is Christ. As Edwards can testify, he

> found, from time to time, an inward sweetness; in what I know not how to express otherwise, than by a calm, sweet abstraction of soul from all the concerns of this world; and a kind of vision, *or fixed ideas and imaginations*, of being alone in the mountains, or some solitary wilderness, far from all mankind, sweetly conversing with Christ, and wrapt and swallowed up in God. The sense I had of divine things, would . . . kindle up a sweet burning in my heart; an ardor of my soul, that I know not how to express.[50]

Jonathan Edwards's experience of contemplation. Contemplation was a central aspect of Edwards's life. When Edwards was young he would use everyday circumstances to focus his contemplation. When viewing thunderstorms, he would "view the clouds, and see the lightnings play, and hear the majestic and awful voice of God's thunder: which often times was exceeding entertaining, leading me to sweet contemplations of my great and glorious God."[51] His life was also ordered around time to spend in contemplation. For Edwards, contemplation entailed the peace that only comes through nature: "I very frequently used to retire into a solitary place, on the banks of the Hudson's River, at some distance from the city, for contemplation on divine things, and secret converse with God; and had many sweet hours there."[52] Like the example of Christ, Edwards would take extended times of solitude to focus on his God.

Contemplation is not an act of self-willing. As with all means of grace, contemplation is taking a posture before God as a receiver of his grace. It is an act of seeking God's gracious power upon one's soul. Edwards describes a time in contemplation when God's power seized him:

> Once, as I rid out into the woods for my health . . . as my manner commonly has been, to walk for divine contemplation and prayer; I had a view, that for me was extraordinary, of the glory of the Son of God; as mediator between God and man; and his wonderful, great, full, pure and sweet grace and love, and meek and gentle condescension. . . . Which continued, as near as I can judge, about an hour; which kept me, the bigger part of the time, in a flood of tears, and weeping aloud.[53]

God revealed the glory of his Son to Edwards as he spent time contemplating him in solitude. The fact that this situation stands out leads us to believe that this was not typical. This activity was common behavior for him, and yet he did not always receive this clear view of Christ in his heart. Ultimately, Edwards did not seek out this particular grace. Rather, he focused his mind and heart on Christ, trusting that Christ was faithful. To understand Edwards's spirituality, one must understand his devotion to contemplation. If contemplating God does not make sense, neither will Edwards. As Edwards describes his spiritual journey, he narrates what drove his spiritual practices. Heaven is the ultimate reason; being *with* God fully drove Edwards's life. As he describes it:

> The heaven I desired was a heaven of holiness; to be with God, and to spend my eternity in divine love, and holy communion with Christ. My mind was very much taken up with contemplations on heaven, and the enjoyments of those there; and living there in perfect holiness, humility and love.[54]

Temptations in contemplation. To conclude, it is important to briefly address the various temptations in contemplation. Edwards outlines several of these. With contemplation particularly, there are many subtle temptations that can take your focus off of God and put it on yourself. It is important to attend to these temptations so your own practice of contemplation will not falter on the same stumbling blocks.

Temptation: The wandering mind. Unlike meditation, contemplation sets the mind away from itself and holds it there. Your mind won't like this. Immediately, you will find your mind wandering and the anxious beliefs of your heart filling your consciousness. When this happens in meditation, it is often fruitful content for soliloquy. In meditation your mind wandering is fodder for being known as you really are before the God who really is.[55] In contemplation, the reaction to mind wandering is to focus your mind more intently. "Don't let us suffer our thoughts to be taken upon with earthly things that are unworthy of them, when we have such glorious themes of contemplation exhibited to us in the Gospel."[56] Ultimately, the greatest good for your mind is to turn it to Christ. Your response, as your flesh revolts at this, is to allow the other thoughts to fade away and to turn to Christ. When you cannot, you can only pray, "I believe; help me in my unbelief" or "Without you, I can do nothing" (see Mk 9:24; Jn 15:5).

Temptation: Diversions. Similar to the first temptation, the temptation for diversion is the result of a soul that has not learned to rest in its Lord. Edwards worried about this reality, not only in contemplation, but particularly after Sunday worship. People leave church after having their minds set on Christ, and they immediately divert them to worldly things. But these times are ideal for focusing our minds on Christ.⁵⁷ Your mind is primed and ready. Instead, we often waste it by moving onto worldly problems and concerns. Think how easy it can be to go to church, hear God's Word and then immediately watch a football game. The seed falls on shallow soil and dies because it has no depth of soil (Mt 13:5). In contemplation, one can often subconsciously seek diversions to avoid the reality of who God is. When our minds wander to things that make us feel better about ourselves, it is a sure sign that our flesh is seeking to protect us from God. These things are nothing more than the bushes and fig leaves in the garden—ways to hide from the presence of God.

Temptation: Focus on oneself. As noted earlier, contemplation focuses on God rather than oneself. That said, you do not disappear. It is still *you* that contemplates God. Therefore you must note what you do with your contemplation of God. Are you humbled when you focus on God? Or, rather, are you prideful? Edwards tells us that a sign of hypocrisy is to focus on your experiences of God and rejoice in those rather than receiving the reality of that experience (namely, something like humility). Instead of focusing on the goodness, graciousness and holiness of God, these persons focus on themselves and their own experiences. Edwards tells us:

> What they are principally taken and elevated with, is not the glory of God, or beauty of Christ, but the beauty of their experi-

ences. They keep thinking with themselves, "What a good experience is this! What a great discovery is this! What wonderful
things have I met with!" And so they put their experiences in
the place of Christ, and his beauty and fullness; and instead of
rejoicing in Christ Jesus, they rejoice in their admirable experiences: instead of feeding and feasting their souls in the view of
what is without them, viz. the innate, sweet, refreshing amia-
bleness of the things exhibited in the gospel, their eyes are off
from these things, or at least they view them only as it were
sideways; but the object that fixes their contemplation, is their
experience; and they are feeding their souls, and feasting a
selfish principle with a view of their discoveries: they take more
comfort in their discoveries than in Christ discovered.[58]

There are, of course, many more temptations in contemplating
God, but these cover the major ones. Each temptation addresses a
different turning away from God and onto yourself. In contemplation, this is the grave error.

CONCLUSION

Meditation and contemplation are at the heart of the Christian life.
Understanding the Christian's calling to set our minds on Christ is a
major step toward understanding how Edwards (and the Christian
tradition) viewed the Christian life. It is no wonder that Edwards
often slipped into poetry when talking about God and his work. He
was truly taken aback by the fullness of God. But God's beauty wasn't
the only beauty that caught Edwards's eye. When Edwards first saw
Sarah, the girl who would become his wife, he wrote a poem about
her. This is helpful for us because, unlike how we might write about
someone we are attracted to, Edwards focuses on her spiritual attrac-
tiveness. In other words, Edwards portrays his future wife as spiritually beautiful. Notice what he focuses on:

They say there is a young lady in [New Haven] who is beloved
of that almighty Being, who made and rules the world, and
that there are certain seasons in which this great Being, in
some way or other invisible, comes to her and fills her mind
with exceeding sweet delight, and that she hardly cares for
anything, except to meditate on him — that she expects after a
while to be received up where he is, to be raised out of the
world and caught up into heaven; being assured that he loves
her too well to let her remain at a distance from him always.
There she is to dwell with him, and to be ravished with his
love, favor and delight, forever. Therefore, if you present
all the world before her, with the richest of its treasures, she
disregards it and cares not for it, and is unmindful of any pain
or affliction. She has a strange sweetness in her mind, and
sweetness of temper, uncommon purity in her affections; is
most just and praiseworthy in all her actions; and you could
not persuade her to do anything thought wrong or sinful, if
you would give her all the world, lest she should offend this
great Being. She is of a wonderful sweetness, calmness and
universal benevolence of mind; especially after those times
in which this great God has manifested himself to her mind.
She will sometimes go about, singing sweetly, from place
to [place]; and seems to be always full of joy and pleasure;
and no one knows for what. She loves to be alone, and to
wander in the fields and on the mountains, and seems to have
someone invisible always conversing with her.[59]

Sarah often took times of solitude to wander in the wilderness
with God, sweetly conversing with him. Sarah had a "calmness of
mind." While this description is certainly one of a love-struck young
man, it is also a description of the ideal Christian existence. Sarah,
in Edwards's mind, was entirely propelled by the God who will one

day reveal himself to her fully. In conclusion of this chapter, therefore, let me focus our attention on this description of spirituality. In particular, it is important to focus on this notion of rest and calmness that we have seen in Edwards's thought.

Alongside Edwards's poem to Sarah is his "Personal Narrative," a description of his spiritual journey. There he offers an important point concerning the nature of holiness. "Holiness, as I then wrote down some of my contemplations on it, appeared to me to be of a sweet, pleasant, charming, serene, calm nature."[60] Holiness has a "calm nature." As such, it brings rest to the soul. This is why he states, "The spiritual enjoyments believers have through Christ are attended with quietness and rest of soul."[61] Rest, as noted above, is not inactivity, but the kind of activity the soul was made for. It is understanding what it means to "Be still, and know that I am God" (Ps 46:10). This, therefore, is the reality of the gift of grace. Against New Age spirituality, calming oneself through self-centering is either impossible or ultimately fruitless. In Christ, we know a true calmness of spirit only as we are confronted with Christ and the knowledge of his call (Mt 11:28-30). Holiness brings about a posture of receiving, just as a posture of receiving is an important step in receiving holiness from God:

> It seemed to me, it [holiness] brought an inexpressible purity, brightness, peacefulness and ravishment to the soul: and that it made the soul like a field or garden of God, with all manner of pleasant flowers; that is all pleasant, delightful and undisturbed; enjoying a sweet calm, and the gentle vivifying beams of the sun. The soul of a true Christian, as I then wrote my meditations, appeared like such a little white flower, as we see in the spring of the year; low and humble on the ground, opening its bosom, to receive the pleasant beams of the sun's glory; rejoicing as it were, in a calm rapture; diffusing around a

sweet fragrancy; standing peacefully and lovingly, in the midst of other flowers round about; all in like manner opening their bosoms, to drink in the light of the sun.[62]

This rest is not idleness.[63] In our glorified state, where the sight of God will be perfectly clear and the soul will be in perfect rest, we will not be idle. God's perfect beauty and glory does not take over our imagination such that we cannot do anything else. Rather, a vision of God creates perfect human society. A vision of God brings about society as it was meant to be because this vision recalibrates our hearts to love. For this society to exist people must have restfulness of heart—they need to be re-collected around who they are in Christ in a perfect manner. Note Edwards's description of this rest:

> Every faculty of the believer is satisfied and at rest in Christ. The understanding rests here, it desires no other object to be its portion, to entertain in contemplation; the glory of Christ is object enough for the entertainment of that extensive faculty. The will and affections are at rest in the beauty and love of Christ; here they are immovably fixed and need no other object to entertain and fill them, and be their everlasting food. The soul of the believer is at rest in Christ, as it desires not a more glorious object, a more sweet and delightful good than Jesus Christ.[64]

Meditation and contemplation will form everything we do in the Christian life. So also, the belief that God's presence brings rest to the soul will form your Christian existence (Zeph 3:17). This is incredibly telling for a person who lived on the edge of the wilderness, with the fear of attack always imminent. Edwards lived in a chaotic age, with war and division always at his doorstep. Just as the spiritual tradition used Mary and Martha as examples of differing postures of the Christian life, so does Edwards seem to use them as types of people. Martha is "worried and anxious about so many things," while Mary is at rest as she sits at the feet of Jesus (Lk 10:38-42). Edwards sought to walk the way of Mary. Walking the way of Mary, which is simply living the way of Christ, shapes us to pray properly. If we are truly re-collected around God in Christ by the Spirit, we come before him as those sweet little flowers—quiet, calm and humble:

> Christ so came like a humble, meek suppliant to the throne of grace with a *quiet, calm, humble, waiting, hoping* disposition. It may be, on the contrary, your petitions were put up with an inwardly *unquiet, turbulent, discontented, unsubmissive* sort of spirit. A prayer that is put up after this manner, is no real prayer. Such persons don't act the part of beggars that supplicate and pray, but of creditors that demand their dues.[65]

Those who have a meek and humble disposition are depending upon God and can trust Zephaniah's proclamation that "The LORD your God is in your midst, / a mighty one who will save; / he will rejoice over you with gladness; / and will quiet you by his love" (Zeph 3:17). Being with Christ is being at rest in him. Those like Martha, "worried and anxious about so many things," cannot find rest in the midst of worldly distractions. Those like Mary are at rest in God's glory, so they are free to be fully alive. Being fully alive is not "being too heavenly minded for earthly good." Rather, being heavenly minded is being the most earthly good, exactly because your mind is set on Christ. Building on this, we turn our attention to the final chapter, looking at the spiritual practices that defined the rhythms of Edwards's life.

Jonathan Edwards's Spiritual Practices

*Christ thus redeemed the elect and purchased grace for them
to that end, that they might walk in holy practice.*

JONATHAN EDWARDS, *CHARITY AND ITS FRUITS*

*I appeal to you therefore, brothers, by the mercies of God,
to present your bodies as a living sacrifice, holy and
acceptable to God, which is your spiritual worship.*

ROMANS 12:1

To UNDERSTAND WHAT WE DO, and why we do what we do,
we must always keep the big picture in mind. This big picture has to
do with the triune God of glory and beauty who has called us into his
own life. That calling entails a life of response. The purpose of this
chapter is to highlight several key "rhythms" (responses) of Edwards's
spiritual life. These are spiritual practices, or means of grace, he em-

ployed throughout his life. We have seen the purpose of means of grace as spiritual postures—ways to be open to the gift of God's grace. The foundation for these are the Word of God and prayer, and building on that, examination, meditation and contemplation. Each of the practices listed below are only understood if they build upon this foundation. These are not ways to fix your problems, nor are they ways to stop sinning. Rather, these practices are ways to be open to the Lord. These are ways we "present ourselves as living sacrifices" (see Rom 12:1) before the Lord. They lead us to a greater knowledge of ourselves so we can be open to the Lord in the midst of our depravity and inability. These tap into our weakness so that we receive the Word of the Lord as Paul did: "My grace is sufficient for you, for my power is made perfect in weakness" (2 Cor 12:9). To continue the image employed throughout this book, these are ways given by God for our hearts to be recalibrated to him. Through these practices and God's grace we continue to "taste and see that the Lord is good" (Ps 34:8).

Edwards was intensely devoted to God. Each of the following practices were assumed as obvious disciplines of the Christian life. In our day, this is not so. For us, therefore, the most important temptation will be to take these practices and use them as ways to grow ourselves. We are often tempted to mine the tradition for "tricks" that can fix our spiritual malaise. Spiritual practices become acts of magic we try to use to fix our lives. This is unhelpful. Rather, these are responses to God's call, postures of weakness and dependence seeking God's power alone. These are means to lay down our lives before him to receive his grace.

We have already looked at prayer, Scripture, examination, meditation and contemplation. These were the core of Edwards's spiritual life. Here, I focus our attention on sabbath, fasting, conferencing, soliloquy, silence and solitude, and prayer (again). These will not be expansive, but are meant to give an overview of several of the spiritual practices that shaped Edwards's life. In the exposition of these practices I follow a simple format. First, there is a brief introduction, followed by the question, Why? Then I address Edwards's own practice and conclude with some notes about our imitation. The overall purpose is to give us a feel for these practices and raise questions as to how we can imitate Edwards as he imitated Christ.

SABBATH

Sabbath is a perfect place to start talking about the rhythms of Edwards's spiritual life. Meditation, contemplation, studying the Word and prayer form the day-to-day realities of life. Sabbath forms the weekly rhythm of life under God. Sabbath is a gift from God for our good (Mk 2:27); it is "an image of the future heavenly rest" for the church (Heb 4:9-11).[1] Sabbath, rather than being a burden, is a sign of God's love.

Why sabbath? Edwards believed that sabbath was a divine commandment for all Christians. It is a day set apart for rest—not only physical rest, but more specifically spiritual rest. We have already seen that rest does not mean inactivity; sabbath is not a vacation. Sabbath is a day a week defined by the recalibration of the soul to its Lord. Other days should include means of recalibration, but sabbath is *defined* by it. As such, it is a day of rejoicing.[2] Sabbath is not only about our spiritual health but is also a sign to the world. Sabbath is the day that our core values take over, where we can set aside the tasks of our work and focus entirely on God. Whereas God's grace might be known through the witness of individuals, the church's devotion to God is seen in her commitment to sabbath.

Edwards's practice of sabbath. Edwards's practice of sabbath had several points of emphasis. First, he focused on sabbath as "holy time."[3] This was time set apart; therefore it was time devoted against the powers of sin and flesh. Sabbath rest entails self-examination and meditation within the grace of God. This is not time to follow rules to prove to God you obey but time to be who you truly are before the

God who is. It is turning to dependence above all. Second, sabbath is a time to put aside the concerns that normally drive your life. We are so inundated by the simple realities of life that they can become ends in themselves. We forget we live in a God-saturated world. Sabbath is a time to set your mind on God alone, so that this carries over throughout your week. Sabbath rest is a reorientation so that your work can be done for the glory of God.

Third, sabbath is a time to focus ourselves on spiritual things. In other words, we devote ourselves to the means of grace. Some of these will be obvious: hearing God's Word preached, possibly taking communion and so on. Others not as much. Edwards suggests reading God's Word and meditating, as well as reading books on the Christian life. Sabbath should abound in "secret duties," that is, private prayer, meditation and reading. But sabbath should also be public as well. This includes meeting with others to encourage one another. One of the practices that would have been typical is "conferencing," which I explain below. Families should practice sabbath together as the church in miniature. Fourth, as all of this is going on, redemption should be the primary focus. Sabbath was given a new meaning by Christ's resurrection. The reality of Christ who put death to death should be received and meditated upon with joy.[4] Last, Edwards encourages works of mercy and charity on sabbath. Sabbath is not a turn to isolation but to love of God and neighbor (Lk 6:1-11). When Edwards calls his people to silence, solitude, meditation and contemplation, this is not a turn inward, but a turning Godward. These are means to set our minds on Christ that we may live as he did.

Imitation. How can we imitate Edwards in his practice of sabbath? First, it is easy to get overwhelmed by the amount of things listed. But this is not a checklist of activities for sabbath keeping. He is not saying that every sabbath must include all of these elements, but that the tenor of sabbath keeping should be oriented by these things.

When you think of what sabbath is about, these things should come to mind. Second, particularly in an age where we are always *plugged-in, connected* and *glued* to our televisions and computers (just think about the words we use to talk about that), we need sabbath. We need a day without logging in, without watching TV and without the burdens and chaos of our overfilled lives. Third, the apostle Paul talked a lot about imitation. If we think of the Christians who walked before us with integrity, holiness and a rich life of faith, they all kept a sabbath. Try to find one that didn't. Sabbath is a mark of people who have given themselves to God. It is not a day of making sure you don't break the rules, but should be a day of utmost freedom. Sabbath is a weekly remembrance that the chains are off. It is a day of joy. Imitate Edwards in celebrating.

FASTING

Fasting has always been a spiritual practice kept by God's people (1 Sam 7:6; 2 Sam 12:16; Neh 1:4; Esther 4:16; Is 58:3-6; Mt 4:2; Acts 13:2-3). For Edwards, along with most of the Christian tradition, fasting was first and foremost a community practice and only secondarily a private practice. In other words, fasting was a practice done by a community seeking God. It was primarily a communal means of grace. Fasting was an opportunity to prepare the hearts of God's people. It is taking on a posture of receiving by embracing our weakness.

Why fasting? Fasting has always been wrought with temptation (Jer 14:12). When Edwards talks about fasting he is quick to note this. He even claims that "in our very fasting" we might make ourselves more "unfit" for grace and mercy.[5] Fasting is not a way to bend God's will to your own; it is not even a way to defeat your flesh. Fasting is a means to prepare your heart. As such, it must be accompanied by contrition of heart. Fasting is creating space in your weakness for prayer, repentance and trust. It is a way to pray "the spirit indeed is willing, but the flesh is weak" (Mt 26:41). In grasping the weakness of being finite you are called to grasp onto God who is infinite. In being a creature whose body needs nourishment, you grasp onto the God who is complete fullness in himself. As such, prayer must saturate fasting. Fasting provides a certain kind of space for prayer. Without prayer, fasting is simply not eating.

Edwards's practice of fasting. In Edwards's time, fast days were integrated in the life of the community. This is true for the church as well as the nation. At this point in history, New England was still really Old England. There was no church/state separation. If the government called for a fast day it was your religious duty to fast. Furthermore, the church would hold its own fasts, often on special occasions based on the church calendar, a death in the community or a natural disaster.[6] Also, Edwards encouraged his people to fast in secret (using Mt 6:16-18). While "secret prayer" should be a daily rhythm, under certain circumstances it is appropriate to add secret fasting. The "special circumstances" were almost always sin. At the heart of Edwards's understanding of fasting was the confession of sins.[7] Prayer in fasting, therefore, is always the prayer of repentance. Fasting was a bodily way of kneeling at the cross, seeking the Savior who gave all for you.

Imitation. With this spiritual practice, it is not intuitively easy to see how we can imitate Edwards. First, we need to keep our health in mind. Edwards often neglected his health when it came to eating. It is important to speak with a doctor about fasting and the state of your health. Second, fast days were integrated in society in a way they are not for us. But we can come up with our own versions of communal fasting, even if it is not necessarily fasting from food. Third, we need to keep in mind the temptations Edwards warns about. Fasting always opens one up to pride, control and a subconscious attempt to cover our depravity. Furthermore, especially in communal settings, fasting can be a means of showing off. Fasting is an opportunity for these subtle vices to come to the surface and is meant to unveil them for repentance. If you fast without discernment, you will simply reinforce these vices rather than expose them. Last, Edwards offers two common errors in fasting: (1) fasting that arises from one's own righteousness and (2) fasting via superstition. The first is fasting out of pride, and the second is seeking to exert effort to move God. The latter is also pride, but in a different form. Edwards warns how these temptations lead to harsh treatment of the body.[8] Fasting should never stem from a belief that the body and bodily desires are inherently evil. The body is not bad. Hungering is not wrong. Fasting, rather, uses weakness to expose the flesh. When pride, control, lust and arrogance arise from your heart, you can hold these before God in repentance.

CONFERENCING

Throughout this book I have focused our attention on the personal rather than communal dimensions of spiritual formation. Here, briefly, we attend to the latter. Community was at the heart of Puritan spirituality. In terms of the means of grace, the key spiritual practice to foster community was called conferencing. We "conference" today, but it is almost always a large group gathering with little real personal interaction. Puritan conference was different. Conference is closest to what we call small groups or maybe accountability partners. That said, it was also much more.

Everyone was expected to have a person to conference with. Whether you were a minister, a farmer, a teenager or a mother of ten, you were to share life with a companion on the journey. This may be in person or through letters (which was seen as less than ideal). Conference was a living interpretation of the "one another" passages in Scripture (for instance, see Rom 12:5, 10; 13:8; Gal 5:13; Eph 4; 5:19; Col 3:16; 1 Thess 4:18; 5:14). In times of conferencing you would talk about Scripture, about the latest sermon you heard and about what was happening in your heart.[9] Furthermore, it was typical for worship to break out of these deeply personal and educational meetings. Edwards addresses Colossians 3:16: "Let the word of Christ dwell in you richly, teaching and admonishing one another in all wisdom, singing psalms and hymns and spiritual songs, with thankfulness in your hearts to God," as explaining public worship *and* conference.[10] One seventeenth-century writer encouraged a friend in a letter:

> If you had a friend with whom you might now and then spend a little time, in conferring together, in opening your hearts, and presenting your unutterable groanings before God, it would be of excellent use: Such an one would greatly strengthen, bestead, and further you in your way to Heaven. . . . Oh! the life of God that falls into the hearts of the Godly, in and by gracious Heavenly conference. Be open hearted one to another, and stand for another against the Devil and all his Angels. Make it thus your business in these and such like ways, to provide for Eternity while it is called today.[11]

Conferencing is grasping the idea that we do not stand under the Word of God alone, but with our brothers and sisters in Christ. Living according to the Word is not an isolated reality but happens in community. What is probably the hardest for us to swallow is the belief that our hearts are not private property but communal property. Freedom in the Christian life comes through being known deeply. Freedom entails both acceptance and continued admonishment and guidance in our life with Christ.

Why conferencing? Living as a pilgrim entails learning to journey well. Likewise, learning to journey well means learning to be a good traveling companion. At the heart of the Christian life is learning to point others to Christ, to bear burdens, to encourage, to love and to be *with* others. In this sense, conference is a spiritual practice designed to flourish every other spiritual practice. Spiritual practices should not be done in isolation, even if they are done alone. All spiritual practices raise up fleshliness to the surface of your heart, even to the point·that you wonder if anything spiritual is actually going on. You are so confronted with your flesh that it often feels like you cannot get beyond that to God. Conference is a time to talk through that, to learn from other's experience and to trust that what you experience in spiritual practice is the result of the Lord's work.

But while we have things like small groups and accountability partners in place for this kind of spiritual conversation, it rarely happens. One of the critiques, no doubt, that Edwards would levy on our modern evangelicalism is that we assume way too much. We assume the Word is sinking into people's hearts in our congregations. We assume that people are living holy lives. We assume that because people give money and volunteer that they must be living in the Spirit. These are bad assumptions. Small groups and accountability groups are not necessarily the answer. Conference was meant, in part, to help secure the Word in the hearts of the congregation. They were not a passive audience. In conference, they poured over the Scriptures and the sermon preached in light of their own souls. They confessed any struggle over the passage or the sermon. They exposed their hardheartedness, their deaf ears and their dull minds. They talked about ways that this truth might form their lives and dialogued with one another how that might come to fruition.

Conference, it is important to note, was not only one-on-one but was also more broadly communal. A meal with friends would turn into conference. Families were expected to have weekly conference together. This was not only to help children navigate their own souls, but to help catechize them according to the sermon heard on Sunday. Children (and parents!) had to do more than just repeat what was said; they had to understand it in light of the whole of God's call for his people. Conference was a key mechanism in the education of Christians. Interestingly, the death of conference has also seen the rise of biblical illiteracy. Conference was understood to be an essential aspect of growing in wisdom. Pastors would model conference through their sermon and in their pastoral counseling. Pastors were trained in wise soul care and were available to admonish those who failed to act gracefully in these settings. In our day, many people sit through legalistic and moralistic self-help principles in small groups and accountability groups without anyone overseeing their leadership. Again, maybe we assume too much?

Conference, furthermore, helped push against an overly internal spirituality with isolationist tendencies. Edwards warns about such people:

> It may be their thoughts will be taken up wholly about religious duties such as praying in secret, reading scripture and good books and going to meeting and giving diligent attention and keeping the Sabbath and meditation. They seem to regard these issues as though they comprised their duty in its full extent, and as if this was their whole work. When moral duties towards their neighbor and their duty in the relations they stand, in their duty as husband or wife or as brother and sister, or their duty as neighbor don't seem to be considered by them. They don't consider the necessity of these things and when they hear of earnestly seeking salvation in a way of diligent attendance on all duties they seem to leave these out of their thoughts as if these weren't meant.[12]

Once again, Edwards refused to assume too much. He refused to assume that the person diligently attending Sunday service, who kept sabbath, meditated and read Scripture and books on the Christian life was actually living out the full breadth of the gospel. We might call this the academic temptation. It is the temptation to fuel the life of the mind and leave the community life to die. The Christian life is reoriented around right belief, and right living is left off as unimportant (or maybe just for other people who care about such things). Note the way Edwards delineates what he calls the two external manifestations of religion:

> But of this inward religion, there are two sorts of external man-ifestations or expressions. The one sort are outward acts of worship, such as meeting in religious assemblies, attending sacraments and other outward institutions, and honoring God with gestures, such as bowing, or kneeling before him, or with words, in speaking honorably of him in prayer, praise, or reli-gious conference. And the other sort are the expressions of our love to God by obeying his moral commands of self-denial, righteousness, meekness, and Christian love, in our behavior among men. And the latter are of vastly the greatest impor-tance in the Christian life.[13]

The means of grace orient us to God and neighbor in love so that by the grace of God we bear the fruit of his Spirit in this world (Gal 5:22-23). This is not simply a mental exercise in right belief, but is an exercise in Christian wisdom.

Edwards's practice of conferencing. Edwards lists conference alongside such practices as public prayer, hearing the Word preached and singing in church (among other things). These were not side issues for Edwards but were at the heart of following Christ. Con-ference was an assumed practice of the Christian life. For a minister, conference would be a continual aspect of weekly ministry.[14] Ed-wards conferenced with fellow pastors both in person and by letter. He led his family in conference weekly, at the very least. He met with congregants for personal conference and led small groups in conference. In doing so, Edwards was modeling something he en-couraged to happen without him.

Every time people come together, there are various temptations that arise. For some, like Edwards, it was easy to digress into debating theology. Edwards warned against doing so in times of conference.[15]

Likewise, Edwards knew from experience how easy it was for pastors to get together and simply talk about worldly things. Talking to pastors, Edwards tells them that instead of spending their time "sitting and smoking, and in diverting, or worldly, unprofitable conversation, telling news, and making their remarks on this and the other trifling subject," that they should "spend their time in praying together, and singing praises, and religious conference. How much do many of the common people shame many of us that are in the work of the ministry in these respects?"[16] It is easy to speak of things that are more socially acceptable than the movements of your heart. It is easier to turn to subjects that you feel control over than to express the areas of your heart that feel uncontrollable. Conference was an action of faith against this temptation.

Imitation. Since we already have small groups and accountability partners in evangelicalism today, it should be relatively easy to bring some principles over from conferencing. First, we need an emphasis on wisdom in conference. Wisdom is a difficult thing; it requires knowledge of God and self, discernment and an experience of living in his grace (Phil 1:9-11). Wisdom requires humility. Second, we need to understand how educationally brilliant conference really is. Think about the difference between listening for your benefit alone and listening because you have to teach someone else. With the former, it is easy to lose focus. With the latter, you take notes and listen well because you want to be able to speak meaningfully when you teach. This is what conference does. Conference is an educational tool because it makes everyone, to some degree, a teacher. You are telling one another what the pastor said, you are searching Scripture to verify and advance his points, and you are navigating the reality of your heart with one another. In doing so the entire congregation comes to wrestle with the truth of God's Word rather than just waiting for someone to tell them what to do. Last, and maybe most foundationally, conference is practice. In conference, we learn to speak about God in humility. This practice should bubble over to the rest of life. Conference is practice to make conversation about God normal.

SOLILOQUY

I have already introduced soliloquy in our discussion of meditation. Therefore I will outline it only briefly here in its own right. If you recall, soliloquy is a practice designed to integrate prayer and self-examination. It is at the heart of the interconnection between our knowledge of God and our self-knowledge. This practice is modeled after various psalms that portray the psalmist's prayer to God and then also to their own soul: "Why are you cast down, O my soul, and why are you in turmoil within me? Hope in God; for I shall again praise him, my salvation and my God" (Ps 42:5-6). As seen here, soliloquy is speaking directly to your soul as you hold it open before the Lord. Soliloquy is a key component in meditation because meditation is not merely focusing one's mind on God but entails wrestling with God's truth as you really are. It entails holding open the truth of yourself and speaking into that truth. Soliloquy is a way to pray "Without you I can do nothing," with a specific aspect of your heart that needs healing. Soliloquy is not an attempt to self-talk your mind into right behavior, nor is it an attempt to come up with an action plan to solve your "sin problems." Rather, soliloquy is prayer. Soliloquy seeks to stand under the Word of God that leaves us "naked and exposed to the eyes of him to whom we must give account" (Heb 4:13). Soliloquy is the opposite of Adam and Eve's hiding from God in the garden, seeking to expose one's heart to God rather than hiding in guilt and shame.

Why soliloquy? Because our knowledge of God depends on knowing who we really are (and therefore knowing our need to repent), the Christian life must take on a posture of complete honesty before God. The Spirit of God given to believers searches the heart

(Rom 8:27) and intercedes from the depths of our hearts (Rom 8:26). The Spirit prays from our spirits about the truth of our brokenness, depravity and sin. The Spirit is not mistaken about who you are. You are the one who is ignorant of your heart. Soliloquy is a practice that acts in faith that the Spirit is searching and praying from your heart, and that, particularly in prayer, he will unveil your own heart to you. Prayer is not just petition, but is an act of being who you really are before God in all his holiness and grace. Prayer is a way of life. Prayer is a posturing of yourself before God in the truth of yourself, so that you can fully grasp the grace he freely gives.

Edwards's practice of soliloquy. Edwards links his practice of soliloquy with his meditation, contemplation, reading of Scripture and prayer. Interestingly, he would also link singing with soliloquy, meditation and prayer, claiming that doing so helps to still the passions and calm the mind. He tells us that "the mind is not fit for such high, refined and exalted contemplations, except it be first reduced to the utmost calmness."[17] Soliloquy depends upon this calmness because it is necessary to assess the "motions" of the mind and heart in prayer. Soliloquy takes what the mind and heart give it—a wandering mind, lustful thoughts, boredom—and uses their momentum against them by holding them before the penetrating glare of God. There is a twofold movement to expose sin and rejoice in God's forgiveness. It is an attempt to uphold both without losing one or the other. The person who forgets the filthiness of sin will find soliloquy pointless. The one who fails to grasp God's grace will either self-talk themselves into a better life (self-help) or will sink into the mire of depression and self-hatred.

Imitation. What might it look like to imitate Edwards in his practice of soliloquy? First, soliloquy is best done when the mind is focused. Therefore, soliloquy is most often employed during meditation, contemplation and lengthy times of prayer. If all you do is pray at God, just before you quickly move on to something else, you will never grasp soliloquy. For Edwards, this was best achieved in nature. Figure out what kind of time and space you need to really calm your mind, so you are not just squeezing prayer into the midst of the everyday chaos of your life. Maybe start by setting aside one hour once a week to sit with the Lord. Trust that the Spirit will unveil the depravity in your heart, and use that depravity to come before the Lord as you really are. If you wish to integrate soliloquy into the core of your spiritual life, like it was for Edwards, then you have to allow this calmness of mind and spirit to be the "neutral" of your life. This is the fruit of dependence upon the Spirit and is not achieved easily. It is the result of a life reoriented by God and his way, so the worries and anxieties of the world do not creep in to create chaos.

Second, there are two errors we need to be aware of. First, it is easy to turn practices like soliloquy into ends in themselves. For instance, soliloquy and self-examination just become about self-exploration. Without the greater end of knowing God, self-knowledge will inevitably lead to very subtle vices like pride, arrogance and independence. Second, it is easy to get stuck in soliloquy rather than keeping it within prayer. In other words, our prayers can digress into self-talk and self-help. Rather than exposing our hearts to God, grasping the reality that we cannot change them, prayer often ceases to be prayer and digresses into inner monologue. Soliloquy is always prayer. The moment soliloquy ceases to be prayer, it ceases to be formational. As a means of grace, soliloquy is a posturing of ourselves before God. This particular posturing is kneeling before the cross with one's heart outstretched to Christ, praying, "Search me, O God, and know my heart! Try me and know my thoughts! And see if there be any grievous way in me, and lead me in the way everlasting!" (Ps 139:23-24).

SILENCE AND SOLITUDE

Silence and solitude were central to Edwards's disciplined life. To have a calm, collected heart and mind, you cannot be overly saturated with the chaos of your busy life. Times of silence and solitude integrated within the weekly rhythms of your life are important to foster the rest necessary to wait on the Lord (Lam 3:24-29). Silence and solitude are not ends in themselves, of course, but are means to greater ends. The benefit is the result of the space created in one's life to be present to the Lord. It is often only in the quiet that God illuminates his presence (1 Kings 19:11-12).

Why silence and solitude? Silence and solitude create space in life to present oneself before the Lord to attend to him and his truth. In a letter to his daughter, Edwards writes, "Retire often from this vain world, and all its bubbles, empty shadows, and vain amuse-ments, and converse with God alone; and seek that divine grace and comfort, the least drop of which is more worth than all the riches, gaiety, pleasures and entertainments of the whole world."[18] "Retire often from this vain world," Edwards tells his daughter. Remove yourself from the chaotic and constant flood of worldliness that you are confronted with on a daily basis (Hab 2:20). Remember that Ed-wards believed we must come to see God as beautiful—the greatest beauty—to really live for him. In his mind, the world was constantly seeking to seduce us with a false beauty. Satan often disguises himself as an angel of light (2 Cor 11:14), we are told, but it would be wrong to suppose that simply means "like an angel." Rather, Satan's dis-guise takes what is ugly and seeks to convince people it is beautiful. Satan takes darkness and markets it as light.

Edwards's practice of silence and solitude. From all accounts, silence and solitude were consistent aspects of Edwards's spiritual life. In his "Personal Narrative," Edwards tells us how he would walk "alone, in a solitary place in my father's pasture, for contemplation,"[19] and that he spent the bulk of his time doing so. Even in childhood, Edwards tells us he "had particular secret places of my own in the woods, where I used to retire by myself; and used to be from time to time much affected."[20] He often talks longingly about "solitary places" and notes how he would "walk alone in the fields" to be with the Lord. Silence and solitude were embodied postures of dependence for Edwards. He did not merely lock himself in his study, but he would walk in the woods. There was a physical detachment from his work and home and a strategic saturation in God's beautiful creation. In nature Edwards heard God speaking through his creation (Ps 19:1-6). To really hear it, he had to cultivate a deep attentiveness to God's world.

Christ is the ultimate example for this practice. "How often do we read," Edwards asks, "of his retiring into mountains and solitary places, for holy converse with his Father."[21] Christ lived in perfect communion with God and would still leave his companions to find a place of solitude to be with his Father. This should be a natural impulse for the Christian. In this sense he tells us, "True religion disposes persons to be much alone, in solitary places, for holy meditation and prayer."[22] Silence and solitude create the right space to be with the Lord in prayer, meditation and contemplation. Since these are central practices of the Christian life, so too are silence and solitude.

Imitation. For us, this is difficult. For many, it may be impossible to find a place to really saturate yourself in God's beautiful creation. For most, though, the issue is not impossibility but a culture of busyness. Christians, maybe even more than most, have adopted a lifestyle that is defined by busyness, chaos and a pressure to stay connected. Edwards's call to us is a call to practice disengagement. Just as it is unnatural for people to live in total isolation, so it is also unnatural for Christians to live without silence and solitude. This is a key difference, Edwards argues, between Christians and non-Christians. Christians "delight to retire from all the world," while non-believers often avoid silence and solitude because it "casts them into melancholy."[23] If you are a Christian who avoids silence and solitude, the question is, why? Have you sold your soul to achievement? Do you find your value in what you get done and therefore cannot put it aside to focus on your Lord? Do you fear the reality of your own heart and therefore fear being alone? Do you fill your life with noise, busyness and distraction to hide from God? The Christian who avoids silence and solitude has much to meditate on, and is the one most called to "retire from this world with all of its vanity."

PRAYER

I have already addressed prayer while outlining the means of grace. Therefore here I will focus on the kinds of prayer Edwards prayed, narrowing our attention on two "kinds": set prayer and ejaculatory prayer. These are, importantly, not the only types of prayer Edwards engaged in. We have already looked at meditation, contemplation and soliloquy, all kinds of prayer. Furthermore, all of our Christian practices are really just different kinds of praying. Edwards strategically devoted himself to prayer—not just "set" or "ejaculatory" prayers, but significant times set apart to be with his Lord.

Why prayer? Edwards makes the fascinating observation that most of the "same expressions that are used in Scripture for faith may be well used for prayer also, such as coming to God or Christ, and looking to him" (Eph 3:12).[24] Likewise, prayer is the "expression of faith." Therefore, Edwards can say explicitly, "Faith in God is expressed in praying to God."[25] Prayer is the bedrock of Christian devotion because it is the natural response to God's supernatural work. Prayer is grasping God himself, rather than seeking to grasp his benefits alone. It is no wonder that David, the man "after [God's] own heart" (1 Sam 13:14) was the great psalm writer. We are called, similarly, to be people after the heart of God, pouring our hearts to him in prayer.

Edwards's practice of prayer. Edwards's life was saturated with prayer. He tells us that "Prayer seemed natural to me; as the breath, by which the inward burnings of my heart had vent."[26] This says much about Edwards's understanding of prayer. He understood prayer as calling us to a particular kind of posture before the Lord. "When you engage in the duty of prayer," Edwards counsels one person, "come to Christ as Mary Magdalene did, Luke 7:37-38. Come and cast yourself down at his feet and kiss 'em, and pour forth upon him the sweet perfumed ointment of divine love, out of a pure and broken heart, as she poured her precious ointment out of her pure, alabaster, broken box."[27] This call to be like Mary, casting ourselves on the grace of God, is a call to allow prayer to form our lives (particularly our devotional lives). In light of this, we turn to two kinds of prayers Edwards devoted himself to: set prayer and ejaculatory prayer.

1. *Set prayers* are set times throughout the day cordoned off for prayer. The main idea behind set prayers is that our lives take on rhythms that set the tone and focus of all we do. For many of us, our lives are defined by rhythms of work, eating, television programming, sports, holidays, shopping seasons and a host of other things that generally have little or nothing to do with God. Set prayers are designed to push back against that reality. These are sanctified spaces carved out in our lives to break out of worldly rhythms and grasp onto heavenly ones (Heb 11:16). That said, Edwards noted that set prayers come with certain temptations. He is particularly concerned over some who become superstitious over the frequency of their set prayers. His advice to his people is that they don't use set prayer "more than twice or at most three times a day." He continues, "Some that have more than ordinary leisure from worldly business may do well to attend it three times a day," and he then goes on to point to the biblical saints who would do so. It is safe to assume that if he is advising his people to do so, he is probably doing so at least as much. Edwards was not one to encourage people to do things he did not do himself.

2. The devotional opposite of set prayers are called *ejaculatory prayers*. Edwards tells us that he was "almost constantly in ejacu-

latory prayer," wherever he was.[28] Ejaculatory prayer is simply praying the desires, frustrations, anxieties, fears, hopes and so forth of your heart in the moment that you feel them. Ejaculatory prayer is learning to converse with God in the everyday (Phil 4:6). In Catholic spirituality, this is called "practicing the presence of God." It is learning to be with the Lord in all things—even the mundane. Or, we might say, it is learning that even what we consider "mundane" aspects of our lives are really saturated with the presence of God. It is taking work, eating, holidays, shopping and so forth and orienting those activities to the glory of God.

Edwards encouraged his congregation to "be frequent in this duty praying with all prayer not only set prayers but in ejaculatory prayer lifting up your heart to God in short and earnest requests when about your work when going by the way and when lying in your bed when you wake up in the night season."[29] In every aspect of your life you should be praying. In his description of his future wife Sarah, we saw that she "seems to have someone invisible always conversing with her."[30] This is his call to his people and to us. In every situation we have someone invisible with us and within us. To "pray without ceasing" (1 Thess 5:17) is to converse with God in the midst of all of our experiences. It is not to filter our prayers, but to pray to God in the midst of our frustrations, pains, angers, joys, elations and so on. It is to pray like the psalmists.

Imitation. Throughout this book we have seen Edwards's devotion to prayer and, hopefully, have felt his prophetic call to be with our Lord in prayer. This should include set times of prayer throughout the day. In Acts we see Peter and John continuing with the set prayers they practiced throughout their lives (Acts 3:1; 10:9). By doing so their lives were continually ordered, not by meals, events or work, but by resting in God. For us, this might mean that we take time, however long, throughout our days to pray. It might just mean taking five minutes at our desks to pray through the Lord's Prayer, meditating on the depth of each passage. It could be taking a psalm or another written prayer to pray through, allowing the words of another to become your own. Or, it might mean that you take the time to pray to God based on whatever is going on in your day. Whatever the case, set prayers can serve as a means to constantly reorient you to God's presence throughout your day. For a Puritan prayer book, let me suggest *The Valley of Vision*, edited by Arthur Bennett (Banner of Truth Trust, 2002), and for a modern Reformed prayer book, see *Seeking God's Face: Praying with the Bible Through the Year*, by Philip F. Reinders (Baker Books, 2010).

In terms of ejaculatory prayer, this serves as a particularly helpful partner with set prayer. While set prayers establish the overall framework of your day, ejaculatory prayers instill in your heart that the Lord is with you in all things. Practicing God's presence throughout your day is coming to grasp Jesus' promise that "I am with you always, to the end of the age" (Mt 28:20). The fruit of abiding in this way is coming to say with Edwards that prayer is like breath. Prayer becomes so natural to you that you bring the Lord into every conversation, emotion, plan and event of your life. Doing so is coming to grasp that prayer and faith go hand in hand.

CONCLUSION

This overview gives you a glimpse into Edwards's spiritual life and what it might look like for us to imitate that. It is necessary to constantly remind yourself of where these practices fit in the overall scope of the Christian life, which is why this chapter was last. There are many dangers and temptations in the Christian life, not the least of which is overemphasizing spiritual practice. Edwards notes that "false religion," which is devotion not built on Christ and his Spirit, "may dispose persons to spend much time in religious duties, such as fasting and long public prayers," and claims it can "make a man willing to spend all his time in religion."[31] This is simply self-help. This is the great danger many fall in when seeking to grow spiritually. Rather, we need to refocus our attention on the broad scope of the spiritual life, understanding that all is to the glory of God. These practices, at their best, are means to taste and see that the Lord is good.

Conclusion

When thou dyest heaven will be no strange place to thee; no,
thou hast been there a thousand times before.

And the city has no need of sun or moon to shine on it,
for the glory of God gives it light, and its lamp is the Lamb.
By its light will the nations walk, and the kings of the earth
will bring their glory into it, and its gates will never be
shut by day—and there will be no night there.

REVELATION 21:23-25

ETERNITY SHOULD CAPTURE OUR IMAGINATION.
The idea that there are people who are "too heavenly minded" to be of any earthy good does not make any sense. Having one's sight caught up to Christ at the right hand of God does not undermine earthly ministry, but empowers it. This life is a journey to eternity. It is a journey that will never cease, but will continue on in the presence of God. One day we will see God "face to face" and will know fully, even as we are fully known (1 Cor 13:12). Our path

is the path of a pilgrim. Our call is to love God and neighbor, to be so captivated by the beauty and glory of God that we bear the fruit of Jesus.

Spiritual formation is how the Spirit of God forms us for this journey. It is the Spirit's work to guide us to desire a better country, the heavenly one (Heb 11:16). Learning to journey well is learning to abide in Christ. It is learning to rest in him. Growing in our ability to travel in this pilgrimage is first and foremost grasping that we are totally unable to do so. Growth is primarily growth in dependence. As such, it is growth in dependence upon both God and our brothers and sisters in the faith. Our journey is not walked in isolation, but in the community of faith.

This journey is wrought with temptation on every side. We are tempted to turn vices into virtues. We use things like pride, power, arrogance and rhetoric to fuel what we call "ministry." We proclaim our neediness and then continue to live from our own power. We advertise our Christian existence through status updates while the secret devotions of our hearts die off. We turn to morality as a way to deal with our sin, depravity and the feeling that we simply are not good enough. We seek to generate a feeling of God rather than seek God himself. We use spiritual practices to leverage God's favor to us. We set our eyes on everything but Christ on the cross, hoping that we can tap into some kind of power to fix our lives.

In contrast, the journey of spiritual formation is a journey of brokenness. It is a journey into the depths of your own heart so that you can grasp onto God more fully. Spiritual formation is a life lived in total dependence upon God, not trading him in for excitement, a platform or greater influence. Spiritual formation is the path less travelled by, because it is shaped by the cross. It is a journey of clarity, where we come to see and know how to live as children of God. For Edwards, this journey was defined by our destination—heaven—

and was therefore characterized by affection, taste and sight. As Christians, we are the ones who have tasted and seen that the Lord is good, and so we grow in tasting and seeing. The spiritual life is ordered by these things. The practices, or postures, of grace are leaning forward with our bodies to taste and see in ways we currently do not. The Christian life is praying, "I believe; help my unbelief." Spiritual formation is being formed for the glory of God. As such, it encompasses all of life: our devotional activities, our families, our missional endeavors and more. Spiritual formation is an orientation of one's heart to God in all things, learning to take on the posture of child before God as Father.

This book is a tool to take you on a journey of wisdom. Wisdom tells us to sit at the feet of our elders rather than the latest ministry fad. What better "elder" than someone who died nearly two hundred and fifty years ago? Wisdom sees through the present temptation to just come up with a right program, whether that program is one of spiritual disciplines, leadership development or pastoral training. Learning to live for the glory of God is not a simple three (or more) step process. Edwards has cast a vision for what it might mean to follow Christ in this world, and that entails continually returning to the height, length, depth and breadth of the gospel. It entails a vision of the triune God of glory and beauty who calls us into his own beauty.

To aid you in your processing, I have attached three appendices to this book. They are "Praying with Jonathan Edwards," "Practicing Conference with Jonathan Edwards" and "Going on Retreat with Jonathan Edwards." Each appendix seeks to lead you into practicing the Christian life according to how Edwards understood it. Practicing these things does not mean you have to agree with everything Edwards thought or said. Rather, it is learning obedience through an elder of the church. In Edwards, we find a figure long upheld by the evangelical church as one of the great spiritual thinkers in our history. In Edwards we find someone that our tradition upholds for his balanced views of the life of the mind and a life of the heart. I hope you will allow Edwards to lead you on a journey of spiritual formation. Above all, I hope you will allow Edwards to point you to the God of beauty. Allow *that* God to capture your imagination.

Appendix 1

Praying with
Jonathan Edwards

In this prayer exercise you will seek to set your mind on Christ. Utilizing meditation and contemplation, as outlined in the book, this exercise leads you on Jonathan Edwards's journey of prayer.

Minimum time: 1 hour

Surroundings: If possible, go into the wilderness, sit overlooking the ocean, walk into a field or find a space in whatever your circumstances that allows you to rest in God's creation.

Verses:

Colossians 3:1-3: "If then you have been raised with Christ, seek the things that are above, where Christ is, seated at the right hand of God. Set your minds on things that are above, not on things that are on earth. For you have died, and your life is hidden with Christ in God."

1 Corinthians 13:12-13: "For now we see in a mirror dimly, but then face to face. Now I know in part; then I shall know fully, even as I have been fully known. So now faith, hope, and love abide, these three; but the greatest of these is love."

Start by reading the Bible passages. With the second passage, read all of 1 Corinthians 13. Ask the Lord to bring rest to your mind and illuminate himself to you so that you can set your mind on Christ. Spend at least fifteen minutes just resting your mind. As thoughts enter your mind, refocus yourself in preparation to kneel before Christ.

Meditation: Meditate on Christ seated at the right hand of God. Read Hebrews 2:14-18, 4:14-16 slowly, meditating on who Christ is for you. Spend at least thirty minutes in meditation and soliloquy.

Soliloquy: As you meditate, what do your mind and heart do? If your mind wanders, hold that open before the Lord. Speak into your soul, "O my soul that is within me, turn to your Lord." Reveal the darkness of your heart and your wandering mind to the Lord. Hold it before him as you continue to meditate on who Christ is for you as your High Priest at the right hand of God. If your soul reacts in disbelief, pray "I believe; help my unbelief!" (Mk 9:24). Do not pretend to have a calmed heart if you do not. Instead, be the person with a hard heart, deaf ears and blind eyes before Christ who is faithful.

Contemplation: Turn your mind to Christ. In light of who you are and who he is, seek his face. In this time, truly know that your High Priest intercedes for you to the Father. Rest in his love.

Praise: Sing your prayers and worship to him.

Appendix 2

Practicing Conference with Jonathan Edwards

This exercise is to help you practice conference as outlined in the book. Choose a partner and use this exercise to start. Once the form becomes familiar to you, feel free to adapt for your own circumstances.

Preparation for Conference:

Frequency: Plan a time to meet weekly.

Location: Find a place where you can talk openly and honestly about what is going on in your life.

Action: Find someone you trust and read the section on conference together. Talk through the importance of confidentiality and what it means to conference well. Come up with a series of questions that you can use to focus your time. Such questions might be: What are you currently learning about God/yourself? In what area of your life are you currently feeling the prophetic glare of Christ? How are you responding? Tell me about your prayer life. Talk to me about the nature of your heart. Is it in chaos or rest? What is your pastor preaching through? What are you learning?

Actual Conference Time:

Pray that the Lord will focus your hearts and that you would be open to seeing yourself more deeply.

Start with the questions you outlined. Focus on your experience of God. As you listen to one another, think about the various temptations outlined in the book. Are you looking to your emotional life as a way to take your spiritual temperature? Are you actually open to seeing your depravity, or do you want something to cover it up? What is your heart's response to unveiling your sin to another? Talk about that. What is your response to hearing someone else's sin? Talk about that.

After you listen and encourage them in the grace of God, pray for one another. Use this time to ask God to enter into each other's circumstances.

Scripture: Talk about the last sermon you heard as a way into a discussion about Scripture and God's call on your life. Discuss what it might mean to incorporate this reality into your life. What kind of posturing before God does this entail? Talk through what it might mean for each of you.

Further questions: Where else does Scripture talk about this? How does it reveal God's character? What is the call on your life? In light of this, what does it mean to be faithful/prayerful? Ask each other about how conference forms your family's prayer life. How should it?

End by having a brief discussion about your friendship and what it might look like for conference to form your relationship. Explore what this might mean for your sphere of relationships.

Appendix 3

Going on Retreat with Jonathan Edwards

This exercise is designed to help you take a private solitude retreat with Edwards. This could be a half-day, full-day, or two days and one night retreat. If you have never done a retreat before, I would suggest starting with a half-day to a full-day retreat.

Time: Take at least three hours (half-day retreat), eight hours (full-day retreat), or two days and one night.

Location: Somewhere quiet. If you are staying overnight, find a retreat center.

Material: Bible, journal, this book.

Before you go: Reread sections on silence and solitude, sabbath, and meditation and contemplation.

Start: Follow the format in appendix one, and use those Scriptures or others.

Throughout your time, your mind might wander aimlessly or you could be overcome with fatigue. If the former, sing through "Be Thou My Vision" and use it as a prayer to focus your mind. As your mind continues to wander, ask the Lord to be your vision, and pray, "I believe; help my unbelief" (Mk 9:24). If the latter, take a nap. Allow yourself to really rest so that you can focus more clearly on

God. Do not see this as a cop-out but as a gift from the Lord.

"Be Thou My Vision"
Ancient Irish; versified by Eleanor Hull, 1912

> Be thou my vision, O Lord of my heart;
> Naught be all else to me, save that thou art;
> Thou my best thought by day or by night,
> Waking or sleeping, thy presence my light.
>
> Be thou my wisdom, and thou my true word;
> I ever with thee and thou with me, Lord;
> Thou my great Father, I thy true son;
> Thou in me dwelling, and I with thee one.
>
> Be thou my battle shield, sword for the fight;
> Be thou my dignity, thou my delight;
> Thou my soul's shelter, thou my high tower:
> Raise thou me heavenward, O Power of my power.
>
> Riches I heed not, nor man's empty praise,
> Thou mine inheritance, now and always:
> Thou and thou only, first in my heart,
> High King of heaven, my treasure thou art.
>
> High King of heaven, my victory won,
> May I reach heaven's joys, O bright heaven's Sun!
> Heart of my own heart, whatever befall,
> Still be my vision, O Ruler of all.

Use: Use this hymn as a prayer to have your sight set on Christ. Let "Be thou my vision" be your prayer for the retreat.

Direction: Focus your time on resting in the Lord, having a calmness of mind and heart, and setting your sight upon him alone. In your journal, write down all of the material that your heart and mind seek to grab on to. Are you tempted to turn this time into an opportunity to accomplish something to prove to the Lord that you are obedient? Or, in other words, are you Martha, anxious and troubled by so many things? Read Luke 10:38-42 as a picture of what you are seeking to do on retreat: you are coming to sit at the feet of Jesus.

Focus your time on meditation, contemplation and rest. Use Psalm 8 as a way to rest in the midst of God's creation.

End with a reflection about the retreat and the motions of your heart. Take time to pray about how the posture practiced on this retreat should form your day-to-day life.

Conference: Consider finding someone to conference with about the retreat.

Appendix 4

The Jonathan Edwards
Project

Reading Jonathan Edwards is not easy. He is a difficult person to read and even more difficult to understand. If you have an interest in reading Edwards, I am hoping I can help. I have started what I call "The Jonathan Edwards Project," which is a series of books that slowly increase in level. The first book is a new edition of Jonathan Edwards's own book *Charity and Its Fruits*, and I conclude that volume with a list of his works in the order I think they should be read. Here is the list of books in the project thus far and a brief note about them:

101 *Charity and Its Fruits: Living in the Light of God's Love*, ed. Kyle Strobel (Crossway, 2012). This introduction to Edwards's work is a new edition of his exposition of 1 Corinthians 13. I provide an introduction, conclusion, definitions of arcane terminology and text-boxes throughout the book that explain difficult concepts. If you want to start reading Edwards, start here.

201 *Formed for the Glory of God: Jonathan Edwards and Spiritual Formation* (InterVarsity Press, 2012). This book, the one you have just read, is the second in the series. It aims to introduce readers to Edwards through his understanding of spiritual formation.

301 To Be Announced.

401 *The Ecumenical Edwards: Jonathan Edwards and the Theologians*, ed. Kyle Strobel (Ashgate Publishing, forthcoming). One common trait among great thinkers is the breadth of their thought and acceptance. Edwards is no different. In this book Roman Catholic, Eastern Orthodox and Protestant theologians put Edwards in conversation with major thinkers from the tradition over a variety of theological topics.

501 *Jonathan Edwards's Theology: A Reinterpretation* (T&T Clark, 2013 — look for the paperback rather than the hardcover). This book is an academic work on Edwards's theology. If you really want to dive into Edwards, this book is for you. That said, this is a serious work of theology. Only read it if you have an interest in academic theology.

For more information about "The Jonathan Edwards Project" and future titles in the series, check www.kylestrobel.com.

Abbreviations

Published Primary Works by Jonathan Edwards

WJE 1   *Freedom of the Will*. Edited by Paul Ramsey. Works of Jonathan Edwards 1. New Haven, CT: Yale University Press, 1957.

WJE 2   *The Religious Affections*. Edited by Perry Miller. Works of Jonathan Edwards 2. New Haven, CT: Yale University Press, 1957.

WJE 4   *The Great Awakening*. Edited by C. C. Goen. Works of Jonathan Edwards 4. New Haven, CT: Yale University Press, 1972.

WJE 5   *Apocalyptic Writings*. Edited by Stephen J. Stein. Works of Jonathan Edwards 5. New Haven, CT: Yale University Press, 1977.

WJE 6   *Scientific and Philosophical Writings*. Edited by Wallace E. Anderson. Works of Jonathan Edwards 6. New Haven, CT: Yale University Press, 1980.

WJE 8   *Ethical Writings*. Edited by Paul Ramsey. Works of Jonathan Edwards 8. New Haven, CT: Yale University Press, 1989.

WJE 10   *Sermons and Discourses, 1720–1723*. Edited by Wilson H. Kimnach. Works of Jonathan Edwards 10. New Haven, CT: Yale University Press, 1992.

WJE 11   *Typological Writings*. Edited by Wallace E. Anderson and David H. Watters. Works of Jonathan Edwards 11. New Haven, CT: Yale University Press, 1993.

WJE 13   *The "Miscellanies": a-500*. Edited by Thomas A. Schafer. Works of Jonathan Edwards 13. New Haven, CT: Yale University Press, 1996.

WJE 14   *Sermons and Discourses, 1723–1729*. Edited by Kenneth P. Minkema. Works of Jonathan Edwards 14. New Haven, CT: Yale University Press, 1997.

WJE 15   *Notes on Scripture*. Edited by Stephen J. Stein. Works of Jonathan Edwards 15. New Haven, CT: Yale University Press, 1998.

WJE 16   *Letters and Personal Writings*. Edited by George S. Claghorn. Works of Jonathan Edwards 16. New Haven, CT: Yale University Press, 1998.

WJE 17   *Sermons and Discourses, 1730–1733.* Edited by Mark R. Valeri. Works of Jonathan Edwards 17. New Haven, CT: Yale University Press, 1999.

WJE 18   *The "Miscellanies": 501-832.* Edited by Ava Chamberlain. Works of Jonathan Edwards 18. New Haven, CT: Yale University Press, 2000.

WJE 19   *Sermons and Discourses, 1734–1738.* Edited by M. X. Lesser. Works of Jonathan Edwards 19. New Haven, CT: Yale University Press, 2001.

WJE 20   *The "Miscellanies": 833-1152.* Edited by Amy Plantinga Pauw. Works of Jonathan Edwards 20. New Haven, CT: Yale University Press, 2002.

WJE 21   *Writings on the Trinity, Grace, and Faith.* Edited by Sang Hyun Lee. Works of Jonathan Edwards 21. New Haven, CT: Yale University Press, 2003.

WJE 22   *Sermons and Discourses, 1739–1742.* Edited by Harry S. Stout and Nathan O. Hatch. Works of Jonathan Edwards 22. New Haven, CT: Yale University Press, 2003.

WJE 23   *The "Miscellanies": 1153-1320.* Edited by Douglas A. Sweeney. Works of Jonathan Edwards 23. New Haven, CT: Yale University Press, 2004.

WJE 24   *The "Blank Bible."* Edited by Stephen J. Stein. Works of Jonathan Edwards 24. New Haven, CT: Yale University Press, 2006.

WJE 25   *Sermons and Discourses, 1743–1758.* Edited by Wilson H. Kimnach. Works of Jonathan Edwards 25. New Haven, CT: Yale University Press, 2006.

Unpublished Primary Works by Jonathan Edwards

WJEO 37   *Documents on the Trinity, Grace and Faith.* Works of Jonathan Edwards Online 37. Jonathan Edwards Center, Yale University, 2008.

WJEO 44   *Sermons, Series II, 1729.* Works of Jonathan Edwards Online 44. Jonathan Edwards Center, Yale University, 2008.

WJEO 46   *Sermons, Series II, 1731–1732.* Works of Jonathan Edwards Online 46. Jonathan Edwards Center, Yale University, 2008.

WJEO 48   *Sermons, Series II, 1733.* Works of Jonathan Edwards Online 48. Jonathan Edwards Center, Yale University, 2008.

WJEO 50   *Sermons, Series II, 1735.* Works of Jonathan Edwards Online 50. Jonathan Edwards Center, Yale University, 2008.

WJEO 51   *Sermons, Series II, 1736.* Works of Jonathan Edwards Online 51. Jonathan Edwards Center, Yale University, 2008.

WJEO 52   *Sermons, Series II, 1737.* Works of Jonathan Edwards Online 52. Jonathan Edwards Center, Yale University, 2008.

WJEO 53   *Sermons, Series II, 1738, and Undated, 1734–1738.* Works of Jonathan Edwards Online 53. Jonathan Edwards Center, Yale University, 2008.

WJEO 57   *Sermons, Series II, January–June 1741.* Works of Jonathan Edwards Online 57. Jonathan Edwards Center, Yale University, 2008.

WJEO 65   *Sermons, Series II, 1747.* Works of Jonathan Edwards Online 65. Jonathan Edwards Center, Yale University, 2008.

WJEO 66   *Sermons, Series II, 1748.* Works of Jonathan Edwards Online 66. Jonathan Edwards Center, Yale University, 2008.

WJEO 68   *Sermons, Series II, 1750.* Works of Jonathan Edwards Online 68. Jonathan Edwards Center, Yale University, 2008.

Notes

Introduction

[1]Henry Scougal, *The Life of God in the Soul of Man*, in *The Works of Henry Scougal*, ed. Don Kistler (Morgan, PA: Soli Deo Gloria, 2002), p. 3.

Chapter 1: A Journey to See Clearly

[1]Jonathan Edwards, "Value of Salvation," WJE 10:324.

[2]I have written on Jonathan Edwards's understanding of the beatific vision in comparison with other Reformed thinkers in "Jonathan Edwards's Reformed Doctrine of the Beatific Vision," in *Jonathan Edwards and Scotland*, ed. Ken Minkema, Adriaan Neale and Kelly van Andel (Edinburgh: Dunedin Academic Press, 2011), pp. 171-88.

[3]Henry Scougal, *The Life of God in the Soul of Man*, in *The Works of Henry Scougal*, ed. Don Kistler (Morgan, PA: Soli Deo Gloria, 2002), p. 23.

[4]Jonathan Edwards, "373. Sermon on Rom. 2:10 (December 1735)," WJEO 50, L. 38v.

[5]Ibid., L. 40v.

[6]Jonathan Edwards, "True Saints Are Present with the Lord," WJE 25:233.

[7]Jonathan Edwards, *Charity and Its Fruits*, WJE 8:386.

[8]Ibid.

[9]Ibid., L. 44v (my emphasis).

[10]Ibid., L. 44v-45r.

[11]Jonathan Edwards, "True Grace, Distinguished from the Experience of Devils," WJE 25:640.

[12]See Jonathan Edwards, "They Sing a New Song," WJE 22:227-44.

[13]Scougal, *Life of God in the Soul of Man*, p. 13.

Chapter 2: Mapping the Way of Love

[1]My friend John Coe, more than anyone else, has taught me the truth that the Christian life is life at the cross, emphasizing that this life is throwing oneself wholly on the grace of God.

[2]For a modern example, see Fred Sanders, *The Deep Things of God: How the Trinity Changes Everything* (Wheaton, IL: Crossway, 2010).

[3]Jonathan Edwards, "The Excellency of Christ," WJE 19:593.

[4]Jonathan Edwards, *The Blessing of God: Previously Unpublished Sermons of Jonathan Edwards*, ed. Michael D. McMullen (Nashville: Broadman & Holman, 2003), p. 177. Furthermore, Edwards states, "For there is doubtless an infinite intimacy between the Father and the Son. . . . And saints being in him, shall, in their measure and manner, partake with him in it, and the blessedness of it." Edwards, "Excellency of Christ," p. 593.

[5]See Greg Peter's chapter, "Spiritual Theology: An Historic Overview," in *A Guide*

to *Christian Spiritual Classics*, ed. Jamin Goggin and Kyle Strobel (Downers Grove, IL: IVP Academic, 2013).

[6]An excellent resource for this theme in Calvin is Julie Canlis, *Calvin's Ladder: A Spiritual Theology of Ascent and Ascension* (Grand Rapids: Eerdmans, 2010).

[7]Jonathan Edwards, "Miscellanies 772: Mediation of Christ," WJE 18:422.

[8]Jonathan Edwards, "Striving after Perfection," WJE 19:692.

[9]"*Communion* with God, however, is distinct from union. Those who are united to Christ are called to *respond* to God's loving embrace. While union with Christ is something that does not ebb and flow, one's experience of communion with Christ can fluctuate. This is an important theological and experiential distinction, for it protects the biblical truth that we are saved by radical and free divine grace. Furthermore, this distinction also protects the biblical truth that the children of God have a relationship with their Lord, and that there are things they can do that either help or hinder it. When a believer grows comfortable with sin (whether sins of commission or sins of omission) this invariably affects the level of intimacy this person feels with God. It is not that God turns from us, but that we run from him. Sin tends to isolate the believer, making him feel distant from God. Then come the accusations—both from Satan and self—which can make the believer worry that he is under God's wrath. In truth, however, saints stand not under wrath but in the safe shadow of the cross." John Owen, *Communion with the Triune God*, ed. Kelly Kapic and Justin Taylor (Wheaton, IL: Crossway, 2007), p. 21.

[10]See Fred Sanders, *The Deep Things of God*.

[11]Jonathan Edwards, "The Subject of a First Work of Grace May Need a New Conversion," WJE 22:191 (cf. 199).

[12]This saying recalls the famous saying of Irenaeus, "The glory of God is man fully alive."

[13]This is what John Piper refers to as Christian hedonism. See his *God's Passion for His Glory: Living the Vision of Jonathan Edwards* (Wheaton, IL: Crossway, 1998), pp. 79-81.

[14]Jonathan Edwards, "348. Genesis 9:12–17," WJE 15:331-32.

[15]Jonathan Edwards, "A Divine and Supernatural Light," WJE 17:424.

[16]Ibid.

[17]Jonathan Edwards, "Miscellanies 724: Preparatory Work," WJE 18:352. Henry Scougal, in his unsurpassable work, *The Life of God in the Soul of Man*, makes a similar point: "He who, with a generous and holy ambition, has raised his eyes towards that uncreated beauty and goodness, and fixed his affections there, is of quite another spirit, of a more excellent and heroic temper than the rest of the world, and cannot but infinitely disdain all mean and unworthy things, and will not entertain any low or base thoughts which might disparage his high and noble pretensions." Henry Scougal, *The Life of God in the Soul of Man*, in *The Works of Henry Scougal*, ed. Don Kistler (Morgan, PA: Soli Deo Gloria, 2002), p. 24.

[18]Jonathan Edwards, *Religious Affections*, WJE 2:298.

[19]Jonathan Edwards, "The Mind," WJE 6:365.

[20]Jonathan Edwards, "Miscellanies 117: The Trinity," WJE 13:284.

[21]Edwards, *Religious Affections*, p. 275.

[22]Ibid., p. 274.

[23]Jonathan Edwards, "Miscellanies 293: Spirit, Creation," WJE 13:384.

[24]Jonathan Edwards, "Concerning the End for Which God Created the World," WJE 8:442.

Chapter 3: Walking in Affection

[1]James K. A. Smith has a discussion of this in his book *Desiring the Kingdom: Worship, Worldview, and Cultural Formation* (Grand Rapids: Baker Academic, 2009). Smith, unfortunately, did not mine the Reformed tradition for material on this matter, which would have proven to be very fruitful for his project.

[2]As Calvin helpfully notes, "From this we may gather that man's nature, so to speak, is a perpetual factory of idols." John Calvin, *Institutes of the Christian Religion*, ed. John T. McNeill, trans. Ford Lewis Battles (Philadelphia: Westminster, 1960), 1.11.8.

[3]Jonathan Edwards, *Religious Affections*, WJE 2:343.

[4]Ibid., p. 120.

[5]"The will, and the affections of the soul, are not two faculties; the affections are not essentially distinct from the will, nor do they differ from the mere actings of the will and inclination of the soul, but only in the liveliness and sensibleness of exercise." Ibid., p. 97.

[6]Ibid., p. 101.

[7]Ibid., p. 100.

[8]Note Calvin who is translating Augustine, "Also, Augustine compellingly contends that in this flesh we never render to God the love we lawfully owe him. He says: 'Love so follows knowledge that no one can love God perfectly who does not first fully know his goodness. While we wander upon the earth, "we see in a mirror dimly" [1 Cor 13:12]. Therefore, it follows that our love is imperfect.' Let us be quite agreed, then, that the law cannot be fulfilled in this life of the flesh, if we observe the weakness of our own nature; as will, moreover, be shown from another passage of Paul [Rom 8:3]." *Institutes*, 2.7.5.

[9]Edwards, *Religious Affections*, p. 118.

[10]Ibid., p. 208.

[11]Ibid., pp. 208-9.

[12]Ibid., p. 114 (my emphasis).

[13]Ibid.

Chapter 4: Spiritual Disciplines as Means of Grace

[1]Dallas Willard argues that grace is not opposed to effort but to earning ("Live Life to the Full," accessed October 24, 2012, http://www.dwillard.org/articles/artview. asp?artID=5). Willard is certainly right. It would be wrong to assume that because grace cannot be earned we do not have to do anything to grow. The Puritan doctrine of "means of grace" was the way they came to outline how we work without earning.

[2]This is basically the Reformed view and was first suggested to me by my friend John Coe.

[3]"What is grace but a principle of holiness? or a holy principle in the heart? This holiness is nothing else but the Spirit." Jonathan Edwards, *Charity and Its Fruits*, WJE 8:298. In Edwards's words, "that holy, divine principle, which we have observed does radically and essentially consist in divine love, is no other than a communication and participation of that same infinite divine love, which is God, and in which the Godhead is eternally breathed forth and subsists in the third person in the blessed Trinity. So that true saving grace is no other than that very love of God; that is, God, in one of the persons of the Trinity, uniting himself to the soul of a creature as a vital principle, dwelling there and exerting himself by the faculties of the soul of man, in his own proper nature, after the manner of a principle of nature." Johnathan Edwards, "Treatise on Grace," WJE 21:194. This is central to Edwards's understanding of the virtuous life. By infusing *love itself* into the person, Edwards has provided the foundation for *every* virtue, which is his argument in *Charity and Its Fruits*. There, he states, "The graces of Christianity are all from the Spirit of Christ sent forth into the heart, and dwelling there as an holy principle and divine nature. And therefore all graces are only the different ways of acting of the same divine nature, as there may be different reflections of the light of the sun. But it is all the same kind of light originally, because it all comes from the same fountain, the same body of light. Grace in the soul is the Holy Ghost acting in the soul, and there communicating his own holy nature." Edwards, *Charity and Its Fruits*, p. 332.

[4]Jonathan Edwards, "Discourse on the Trinity," WJE 21:122.

[5]Jonathan Edwards, "950. Sermon on Prov. 6:22(c) (1750)," WJEO 68.

[6]Ibid.

[7]Ibid.

[8]Jonathan Edwards, "John 5:1-4," WJE 24:934.

[9]Jonathan Edwards, "368. John 2:1-10," WJE 15:359.

[10]Jonathan Edwards, "Miscellanies 539: Means of Grace," WJE 18:85.

[11]These three are heavily paraphrased, but I do believe they provide a helpful gloss on Edwards's own points. See ibid.

[12]Ibid., p. 88.

[13]Jonathan Edwards, *Religious Affections*, WJE 2:121.

[14]Ibid., p. 422.

[15]This was established by Richard Rogers. See O. R. Johnston, "The Means of Grace in Puritan Theology," in *The Evangelical Quarterly* 25, no. 4 (1953): p. 203.

[16]Jonathan Edwards, "854. Sermon on Heb. 6:7 (January 1747)," WJEO 65.

[17]Edwards, "Miscellanies 539: Means of Grace," p. 85.

[18]Ibid., p. 88.

[19]Note Edwards's emphasis: "Every Christian family ought to be as it were a little church, consecrated to Christ, and wholly influenced and govern by his rules. And family education and order are some of the chief of the means of grace. If these fail, all other means are like to prove ineffectual." Jonathan Edwards, "A Farewell Sermon," WJE 25:484. It is amazing that Edwards puts this much emphasis on the life of the family, but, in many ways, the Puritans took the seriousness that the Catholic church put on the monastic life and applied that wholesale to the Christian family. The family was seen as the main place of discipleship.

[20]Jonathan Edwards, "097. Sermon on Ex. 20:24 (1729)," WJEO 44.

[21]Jonathan Edwards, "Graces of the Spirit," WJE 25:285 (my emphasis).

[22]Jonathan Edwards, "A Divine and Supernatural Light," WJE 17:417.

[23]Edwards, "097. Sermon on Ex. 20:24," p. 44 (my edits).

[24]Jonathan Edwards, "Types," WJE 11:152.

[25]Jonathan Edwards, "Miscellanies 1338: Necessity of Revelation," WJE 23:350.

[26]Jonathan Edwards, "Miscellanies 476: Conversion. Faith," WJE 13:522.

[27]Jonathan Edwards, "The Terms of Prayer," WJE 19:787.

[28]Michael Haykin, *Jonathan Edwards: The Holy Spirit in Revival*, p. 146. Quoted in Peter Beck, *The Voice of Faith: Jonathan Edwards's Theology of Prayer* (Guelph, ON: Joshua Press, 2010), p. 141.

[29]See Jonathan Edwards, "Hypocrites Deficient in the Duty of Prayer," Sermon Index.net, accessed September 21, 2012, www.sermonindex.net/modules/articles/index.php?view=article&aid=3393.

[30]Jonathan Edwards, "An Humble Attempt," WJE 5:315-17.

[31]Edwards, "Terms of Prayer," p. 787.

[32]See Edwards, "Hypocrites Deficient."

[33]Jonathan Edwards, "Youth and the Pleasures of Piety," WJE 19:85.

[34]Jonathan Edwards, "That We Ought to Make Religion Our Present and Immediate Business," in *The Blessing of God: Previously Unpublished Sermons of Jonathan Edwards*, ed. Michael D. McMullen (Nashville, TN: Broadman & Holman Publishers, 2003), p. 105.

[35]Jonathan Edwards, "The Most High a Prayer-Hearing God," sermon on Ps. 65:2 #374, WJEO 51 (1736).

[36]Ibid.

[37]Jonathan Edwards, "God's Manner Is First to Prepare Men's Hearts and Then to Answer Their Prayers," in *The Glory and Honor of God: Previously Unpublished Sermons of Jonathan Edwards*, ed. Michael D. McMullen, vol. 2 (Nashville, TN: Broadman & Holman Publishers, 2004), p. 81.

[38]Ibid., p. 105.

[39]Ibid.

[40]Edwards, "Terms of Prayer," p. 787 (my emphasis).

[41]Jonathan Edwards, "Faith," WJE 21:439.

[42]Edwards, "Terms of Prayer," p. 786.

[43]Ibid., p. 787.

[44]Jonathan Edwards, "Diary," WJE 16:778.

[45]See Edwards, "Hypocrites Deficient."

CHAPTER 5: KNOWLEDGE OF GOD AND KNOWLEDGE OF SELF

[1]John Calvin, *Institutes of the Christian Religion*, ed. John T. McNeill, trans. Ford Lewis Battles (Philadelphia: Westminster, 1960), 1.1.1.

[2]Ibid., 1.1.2.

[3]"There can be no true humility in any without the creature's seeing his distance from God, not only with respect to greatness but also loveliness. The angels and saints in heaven see both. They see not only how much greater God is than they,

but how much more lovely he is than they. So that though they have no absolute deformity and filthiness as fallen man has, yet as compared with God it is said the heavens are not pure in his sight, and his angels he charges with folly (Job 15:15; 4:18). From such a sense of their own comparative meanness persons are made sensible how unworthy they are of God's mercy or gracious notice. Such a sense Jacob expressed, Genesis 32:10, 'I am not worthy of the least of all the mercies, and of all the truth, which thou hast showed unto thy servant.' And David, 'Who am I, and what is my house, that thou hast brought me hitherto' (2 Samuel 7:18)? And 1 Chronicles 29:14, 'Who am I, and what is my people, that we should be able to offer so willingly after this sort?'" Jonathan Edwards, *Charity and Its Fruits*, WJE 8:237.

[4]Ibid., p. 135.

[5]Jonathan Edwards, "Duty of Self-Examination," WJE 10:488.

[6]Jonathan Edwards, "True Grace, Distinguished from the Experience of Devils," WJE 25:637.

[7]Ibid.

[8]Jonathan Edwards, *Religious Affections*, WJE 2:325.

[9]Edwards, *Charity and Its Fruits*, p. 234.

[10]Ibid., p. 237.

[11]Jonathan Edwards, "Personal Narrative," WJE 16:802.

[12]Ibid.

[13]Edwards, *Religious Affections*, pp. 324, 328.

[14]Edwards, "Personal Narrative," p. 803.

[15]Ibid.

[16]Ibid.

[17]Jonathan Edwards, "Personal Writings: Introduction," WJE 16:742.

[18]Jonathan Edwards, "Resolutions," WJE 16:753.

[19]Edwards, "Personal Narrative," p. 795 (my emphasis).

[20]Ibid.

[21]Note that the author of Hebrews moves from the sword of the Spirit cutting and piercing us to Christ's office of priest.

[22]When making judgment calls, especially *theological* judgment calls, we have to maintain a posture of humility. Note Edwards's emphasis against judging others: "The many texts against judging. Proverbs 26:12, 'Seest thou a man wise in his own conceit? There is more hope of a fool than of him.' Isaiah 5:21, 'Woe to them that are wise in their own eyes, and prudent in their own sight.' Isaiah 65:5, 'Which say, Stand by thyself; come not near to me. For I am holier than thou.' Luke 18:9, Luke 18:11, the Pharisees 'trusted in themselves that they were righteous, and despised others; they thanked God that they were not as other men.' Romans 2:17-20, 'Thou makest thy boast of God, and knowest his will, and approvest the things that are more excellent, and art confident that thou thyself art a guide of the blind, a light of them which are in darkness, an instructor of the foolish, a teacher of babes.' 1 Corinthians 8:2, 'If any man thinks he knoweth anything, he knoweth nothing yet as he ought to know.' 1 Corinthians 13:4, 'Charity vaunteth not itself, is not puffed up, doth not behave itself unseemly.'

Ephesians 5:21, 'submitting yourselves, one to another, in the fear of God.' James 3:1, 'Be not many masters.' James and John were for calling for fire from heaven on the Samaritans, because they would not receive them into their villages. But Christ rebuked 'em, and told 'em they knew not what manner of spirit they were of. Romans 12:18, 'If it be possible, as much as lieth in you, live peaceably with all men.' Philippians 4:5, 'Let your moderation be known unto all men.' 1 Corinthians 9:19, 'For though I be free from all men, yet I made my servant unto all, that I might gain the more'; so 1 Corinthians 9:20-22. 1 Corinthians 10:32-33, 'Giving none offense, neither to the Jews, nor to the Gentiles, nor to the church of God. Even as I please all men in all things, not seeking mine own profit, but the profit of many, that they may be saved'; so Romans 15:2-3. Matthew 18:15, 'If thy brother trespass against thee go and tell him his fault between thee and him alone.' 1 Corinthians 3:4, 'For while one saith, I am of Paul, and [another,] I [am] of Apollos, are ye not carnal?' 1 Thessalonians 4:11, 'That ye study to be quiet and do your own business.' 1 Timothy 5:13, 'They learn to be idle, wandering about from house to house, and not only idle, but tattlers also and busybodies, speaking things which they ought not.' 2 Thessalonians 3:11-12, 'For we hear that there are some which walk among you disorderly, working not at all, but are busybodies. Now them that are such we command and exhort by our Lord Jesus Christ, that with quietness they work and eat their own bread.' Colossians 4:5-6, 'Walk in wisdom towards those that are without, redeeming the time. Let your speech be always with grace, seasoned with salt, that ye may know how ye ought to answer every man.' 1 Thessalonians 4:11, 'That ye study to be quiet, and to do your own business, and to work with your own hands, as we commanded you.' Gen. [*sic*] Genesis 23:11-12, 'Abraham stood up, and bowed himself to the people of the land.' Genesis 33:3, 'Jacob bowed himself to the ground seven times, until he came near to his brother Esau.' Matthew 5:47, 'If ye salute your brethren only, what do ye more than others? Do not even the publicans so?' Acts 26:25, 'I am not mad, most noble Festus.' Paul was gentle and sweet towards the rough soldiers that were for killing him (Acts 27:21–42)." Jonathan Edwards, "Miscellanies 989: Humility," WJE 20:313-14.

23We have to be exceedingly careful to inspect how we see ourselves before God and others. Edwards admonishes: "A poor man is modest in his speech and behavior; so, and much more, and more certainly and universally, is one that is poor in spirit; he is humble and modest in his behavior amongst men. 'Tis in vain for any to pretend that they are humble, and as little children before God, when they are haughty, assuming and impudent in their behavior amongst men. The Apostle informs us that the design of the gospel is to cut off all glorying, not only before God, but also before men (Romans 4:1-2). Some pretend to great humiliation, that are very haughty, audacious and assuming in their external appearance and behavior: but they ought to consider those scriptures, Psalms 131:1. 'Lord, my heart is not haughty, nor my eyes lofty; neither do I exercise myself in great matters, or in things too high for me.' Proverbs 6:16-17, 'These six things doth the Lord hate, yea seven are an abomination unto him; a proud look,' etc. Ch. 21:4, 'An high look, and a proud heart, are sin.' Psalms 18:27, 'Thou wilt bring down high looks.' And Psalms 101:5, 'Him that hath an high look, and a proud heart, will I not suffer.' I Corinthians 13:4, 'Charity vaunteth not itself; doth not behave itself unseemly.' There is a certain amiable modesty and fear that belongs to a Christian behavior among men, arising from humility that the Scriptures often speaks of; I Peter 3:15, 'Be ready to give an answer to every man that asketh you . . . with meekness and fear.' Romans 13:7, 'Fear, to whom fear.' II Corinthians 7:15, 'Whilst he remembered the obedience of you all, how with fear and trembling ye received him.' Ephesians 6:5, 'Servants be obedient to them which are your masters according to the flesh, with fear and trembling.' I Peter 2:18, 'Servants be subject to your masters, with all fear.' I Peter 3:2, 'While they behold your chaste conversation, coupled with fear.' I Timothy 2:9, 'That women adorn themselves in modest apparel, with shamefacedness and sobriety.' In this respect a Christian is like a little child; a little child is modest before men, and his heart is apt to be possessed with fear and awe amongst them." Edwards, *Religious Affections*, pp. 337-38.

[24]This point was first instilled in me by my friend John Coe. I think he is right—this is at the heart of the Reformed impulse.

[25]Edwards, "Duty of Self-Examination," p. 491.

[26]In Edwards's words, "Thus, all of our actions ought to be strictly examined and tried, and not only barely to consider the outward action as it is in itself: but also from what principle our actions do arise from; what internal principle we act and live [by], for actions are either good or bad according to the principle whence they arise." Ibid., p. 488.

[27]Jonathan Edwards, "The Threefold Work of the Holy Ghost," WJE 14:387.

[28]Ibid., p. 388.

[29]Jonathan Edwards, "595. Sermon on Matt. 11:12b (February 1741)," WJEO 57.

[30]Jonathan Edwards, "Letter to Deborah Hatheway," WJE 16:94.

[31]Jonathan Edwards, "The Distinguishing Marks," WJE 4:285 (I have changed "shew" to "show").

[32]See Edwards, *Charity and Its Fruits*, p. 194.

CHAPTER 6: MEDITATION AND CONTEMPLATION

[1]Thomas Manton, "Sermon Upon Genesis 24:63," in *The Works of Thomas Manton*, 17:272, quoted in Joel R. Beeke, *Puritan Reformed Spirituality: A Practical Theological Study from Our Reformed and Puritan Heritage* (Darlington, UK: Evangelical Press, 2006), p. 79.

[2]Isaac Ambrose, *Media* (1657), p. 216, quoted in Tom Schwanda, "Soul Recreation: Spiritual Marriage and Ravishment in the Contemplative-Mystical Piety of Isaac Ambrose" (PhD diss., Durham University, 2009), p. 167. According to Schwanda, "During the seventeenth-century contemplation was defined as 'the action of beholding, or looking at with attention and thought.' Similarly Ambrose declares, '[w] hat, shall he ascend, and shall not we in our contemplations follow after him? gaze, O my soul, on this wonderful object, thou needest not feare any check from God or Angel, so that thy contemplation be spiritual and divine.'" Schwanda, "Soul

Recreation," p. 102, quoting Ambrose, *Looking Unto Jesus*, pp. 871-72. For a general overview of Puritans on meditation, see Beeke, *Puritan Reformed Spirituality*, pp. 73-100; Schwanda, "Soul Recreation," pp. 164-216; and U. Milo Kaufmann, *The Pilgrim's Progress and Traditions in Puritan Meditation* (New Haven, CT: Yale University Press, 1966).

[3]Because of the lack of material in Edwards's work depicting meditation specifically, I have provided a broad and rough depiction, mostly taken from Baxter's *The Saints' Everlasting Rest*. It would be wrong, in my opinion, to put too strict a view on Edwards and assume he followed it wholesale. What I have provided here is a broad enough framework that Edwards would have, if nothing else, accepted this as a viable model.

[4]In a sermon on 1 Cor 2:14, Edwards says that "Other knowledge is gotten by thought and meditation, yea, and so is spiritual knowledge; that is, although it is given by God's Spirit, 'tis given commonly in times of meditation and by meditation." Jonathan Edwards, "A Spiritual Understanding of Divine Things Denied to the Unregenerate," WJE 14:95.

[5]Beeke, *Puritan Reformed Spirituality*, p. 76; Schwanda, "Soul Recreation," p. 168.

[6]Jonathan Edwards, "Diary," WJE 16:789.

[7]Jonathan Edwards, "The Justice of God in the Damnation of Sinners," WJE 19:350.

[8]Beeke, *Puritan Reformed Spirituality*, p. 75.

[9]Schwanda, "Soul Recreation," p. 168.

[10]Jonathan Edwards, "Types," WJE 11:152. Note his emphasis: "We should improve to learn the all-sufficiency of God: it appears both in the works of nature and the works of grace, and the book of nature and the book of grace [and] of revelation both teach us a lesson. We should therefore read in both of them." Jonathan Edwards, "God's All-Sufficiency for the Supply of Our Wants," WJE 14:482.

[11]Jonathan Edwards, "Living Peaceably with One Another," WJE 14:118.

[12]Jonathan Edwards, "475. Exodus 25:23–40," WJE 15:573.

[13]Jonathan Edwards, "Perpetuity and Change of the Sabbath," WJE 17:249.

[14]Jonathan Edwards, "Nothing upon Earth Can Represent the Glories of Heaven," WJE 14:156.

[15]Edwards, "A Spiritual Understanding," p. 95.

[16]Jonathan Edwards, "Profitable Hearers of the Word," WJE 14:246.

[17]Edwards, "Diary," p. 781.

[18]Schwanda, "Soul Recreation," p. 178.

[19]Jonathan Edwards, "The Threefold Work of the Holy Ghost," WJE 14:430.

[20]Ibid., p. 431.

[21]Ibid.

[22]Ibid.

[23]Ibid., p. 432.

[24]Ibid.

[25]Ibid.

[26]Ibid.

[27]Ibid., p. 433.

[28]Jonathan Edwards, "Perpetuity and Change," p. 249.

[29]Jonathan Edwards, "437. Sermon on Cant. 5:3-6 (July 1737)," WJEO 52 (author's edits).

[30]Edwards, "A Spiritual Understanding," p. 95.

[31]Edwards, "Diary," pp. 781-82.

[32]Ibid., pp. 778-79.

[33]Jonathan Edwards, "147. Sermon on Is. 5:20 (1729)," WJEO 44.

[34]Jonathan Edwards, Religious Affections, WJE 2:130.

[35]Jonathan Edwards, "895. Sermon on Luke 9:30-31 (April 1748)," WJEO 66.

[36]Ibid.

[37]Jonathan Edwards, "Christ's Example," WJE 21:517-18.

[38]Jonathan Edwards, "219. Sermon on Jer. 10:16," WJEO 46.

[39]Oxford English Dictionary, 17:811; quoted in Schwanda, "Soul Recreation," p. 102.

[40]Edwards, Religious Affections, pp. 422-23.

[41]Jonathan Edwards, "950. Sermon on Prov. 6:22(c) (1750)," WJEO 68.

[42]Jonathan Edwards, "419. Sermon on John 13:23 (January 1737)," WJEO 52.

[43]Jonathan Edwards, "483. Sermon on Ps. 23:2 (July 1738)," WJEO 53.

[44]Edwards, Religious Affections, pp. 252-53.

[45]Jonathan Edwards, "419. Sermon on John 13:23 (January 1737)," WJEO 52 (author's edits).

[46]Edwards, "Personal Narrative," p. 793.

[47]Jonathan Edwards, Freedom of the Will, WJE 1:146.

[48]Jonathan Edwards, "The Mind," WJE 6:374.

[49]Jonathan Edwards, "The Distinguishing Marks," WJE 4:236.

[50]Jonathan Edwards, "Personal Narrative," WJE 16:793 (author's edits and emphasis).

[51]Ibid., p. 794.

[52]Ibid., p. 797.

[53]Ibid., p. 801.

[54]Ibid., p. 795.

[55]My friend John Coe rightfully focuses on this aspect of spiritual formation. Often, we immediately turn to beating ourselves up over our mind's wandering, thinking that our role is to just "fix it." This is simply self-help. Rather, our call is to be who we really are before God so that he can address our fleshliness.

[56]Jonathan Edwards, "118. Sermon on Cant. 8:1 (1729)," WJEO 44.

[57]Jonathan Edwards, "Heeding the Word, and Losing It," WJE 19:52.

[58]Edwards, Religious Affections, pp. 251-52.

[59]Jonathan Edwards, "On Sarah Pierpont," WJE 16:789-90.

[60]Edwards, "Personal Narrative," p. 796.

[61]Jonathan Edwards, "483. Sermon on Ps. 23:2 (July 1738)," WJEO 53.

[62]Edwards, "Personal Narrative," p. 796.

[63]See Edwards, "Perpetuity and Change," pp. 248-50.

[64]Jonathan Edwards, "283. Sermon on Cant. 2:3(a) (1733)," WJEO 48.

[65]Edwards, "Diary," p. 787 (my emphasis).

CHAPTER 7: JONATHAN EDWARDS'S SPIRITUAL PRACTICES

[1] Jonathan Edwards, "Perpetuity and Change of the Sabbath," WJE 17:242-43.

[2] Ibid., p. 243.

[3] Ibid., p. 249.

[4] Ibid.

[5] Jonathan Edwards, "352. Sermon on Ps. 10:17 (March 1735)," WJEO 50.

[6] As an example, see Jonathan Edwards, "Unpublished Letter of May 30, 1735," WJE 4:110, and "Preface by William Cooper," WJE 4:217.

[7] Jonathan Edwards, "Fast Days in Dead Times," WJE 19:74.

[8] Ibid.

[9] The standard work on conference is Joanne J. Jung, *Godly Conversation: Rediscovering the Puritan Practice of Conference* (Grand Rapids: Reformation Heritage Books, 2011).

[10] Jonathan Edwards, "Colossians 3:16," WJE 24:1117.

[11] Jonathan Mitchel, "Letter to a Friend," appended to *A Discourse of the Glory* (London: Printed for Nathaniel Ponder, 1677), pp. 15-16, quoted in Jung, *Godly Conversation*, pp. 12-13.

[12] Jonathan Edwards, "297. Sermon on Ps. 139:23-24 (September 1733)," WJEO 48.

[13] Jonathan Edwards, "Some Thoughts Concerning the Revival," WJE 4:522-23.

[14] Jonathan Edwards, "Letter to the Reverend James Robe," WJE 16:278.

[15] Edwards, "Some Thoughts," p. 431.

[16] Ibid., p. 507.

[17] Jonathan Edwards, "Miscellanies w: Tone," WJE 13:75.

[18] Jonathan Edwards, "Letter to Mary Edwards," WJE 16:289-90.

[19] Jonathan Edwards, "Personal Narrative," WJE 16:793.

[20] Ibid., p. 791.

[21] Jonathan Edwards, *Religious Affections*, WJE 2:374.

[22] Ibid.

[23] Jonathan Edwards, "950. Sermon on Prov. 6:22(c) (1750)," WJEO 68.

[24] Jonathan Edwards, "Faith Notebook," WJE 21:438-39.

[25] Ibid., p. 439.

[26] Edwards, "Personal Narrative," p. 794.

[27] Jonathan Edwards, "Letter to Deborah Hatheway," WJE 16:93.

[28] Edwards, "Personal Narrative," p. 794.

[29] Jonathan Edwards, "595. Sermon on Matt. 11:12(b) (February 1741)," WJEO 57.

[30] Edwards, "On Sarah Pierpont," WJE 16:789-90.

[31] Jonathan Edwards, "Affections Notebook 'No. 7,'" WJEO 37.

METAmorpha.com

Metamorpha Ministries is a spiritual formation ministry with a particular focus on articulating a distinctively *evangelical* understanding of the Christian life. Reaching back through our tradition to mine robustly Protestant and spiritual resources, Metamorpha seeks to proclaim the depths of the Gospel for a lived existence before the face of God. Our resources seek to be biblically, theologically, and spiritually informed, such that Christ never ceases to be the center.

In addition, Metamorpha.com is a ministry resource: for pastors, to help them live and lead in a healthy way in dependence upon Christ; for churches, to help them create communities of people growing in grace; and for individuals who are on a journey with Christ, to encourage, guide, and nurture an openness to the call of Christ on their lives.